20th century type [remix]

20th century type [remix]
written by lewis blackwell
designed by angus hyland
published by gingko press

# 20th century type

## remix

# Contents

# type production has gone mad, with its senseless outpouring of new  types... only in degenerate times can  personality (opposed to the nameless masses) become the aim of human development.

**Jan Tschichold** in *The New Typography*, 1928[1]

"All the old fellows stole our best ideas." **Frederic Goudy** 1865–1947 TIME AND DATE UNKNOWN

"It is not for the purpose of reviving old or making new rules that these facsimiles have been reproduced. One might as well try to provide models for unalterable fashions in garments, houses, furniture, or decoration. However pleasing a new fashion may be, that pleasure does not entirely suppress the desire for change, and that desire was never greater than it is now."
**Theodore Low De Vinne,** in the preface to *A Treatise On Title Pages*, 1902.

## Letters of introduction

We are postliterate – reading images, sounds
and touch – and we create a multimedia language
from an engine devised for typography.
You and me, now and tomorrow

Type design is rarely, if ever, about being wholly original.
At root, there is the need to conform to a great tradition of
letterforms, a tradition which enables us to have the notion of
a readable alphabet. And yet, a totally unreadable font driven
out of the familiar territory of a keyboard is created within the
context of language-making tools. Something familiar through
which we know our instructions are being codified, our orders
remembered. Forget the book, the magazine, or the television
– they are secondary realizations of typography. It is the
keyboard and screen that are our typographic mediators
now, and our typographic intelligence is bonded with that
of computers.

It is an intelligence that is increasingly shared: the spread of
personal computers has not only empowered more people
to make typographic decisions, but has also transformed
the context for producing type designs. The feeding out
of typographic control and information into the broad
community is inevitably shaping a revised sensibility
of typography.

Type is about much more than questions of legibility or
readability. Fashions and technological change are just part
of the backdrop. What makes typography fascinating, and
an essential enquiry for anybody involved in design, is that
this activity is a manifestation of our search for greater
efficiency and greater power in the written word. It reveals
personalities, politics, and economic factors, along with
advances in science. It is a celebration of humanity, and
a vital and subtle indicator of values.

To read the data assembled from our excavation of
typographic history only in the terms that come easily to mind
now, obscures the complexity of matters past, as well as
present. To do so is the opposite of the true aim of historical
enquiry, and yet every history ends up at such a point if it is
ever to be published. This book does more than a little
obscuring of this and misrepresentation of that, being both
short, heavily illustrated (by a minuscule fraction of the
production it purports to cover) and deliberately weighted to
noting the avant-garde rather than the living traditions of
design. It is a primer to prompt research, a tool for probing
notions of the past and present, and a basic scrapbook for
experimentation in the practice of graphic design. It uses an
earlier book, *20th-Century Type*, and remixes its view of the
past with a new present... and invites the reader to remix
again, refining or adding through interrogation and play.
There is an illusion of wholeness with a book, an illusion you
don't have with speech or a website. I ask: how much
smaller or larger should this book be?

There is a 22-character alphabet at the beginning of Sir
Thomas More's *Utopia*, a book first published in Latin in
1516. This alphabet is that of the Utopians, a people who are
so perfectly organized in all things that they are completely
happy. The alphabet is based on the circle, square and
triangle.

There are around sixty-five thousand different characters in
the Unicode worldwide standard for multilingual information. **p.7**

# build a book like a body moving in space and time, like a dynamic relief in which every page is a surface carrying shapes, and every turn of a page a new crossing to a new stage of a single structure.

El Lissitsky, 1920[2]

"In order for language to function, signs must be isolable one from another (otherwise they would not be repeatable). At every level (phonetic, semantic, syntactic, and so on) language has its own laws of combination and continuity, but its primary material is constructed of irreducible atoms (phonemes for spoken language, and for written, signs...)... Language is a hierarchical combination of bits." **Bits of Yve Alain-Bois** in *Formless* (Zone Books, 1997)[3]

Typography fostered the modern idea of individuality, but it destroyed the medieval sense of community and integration.
**Neil Postman,** *Amusing Ourselves To Death*, 1985[4]

This figure is arrived at by counting all the unique characters contained within different languages. This 1990s development, still continuing, supports technology (including fonts) that will enhance the readability of digital documents across devices around the world. At least machines may speak the same language.

Reading might be described as a linear activity. You read along a line. And this travelling along the line of characters, which we form into words and sentences and paragraphs and big thoughts, this pursuit is at the core of our rational process; it is at the heart of much of our information retrieval and analysis. But some writers suggest it was once more so, in the past. Now, whole cultures have long taken their mass-communications from television, or radio, ahead of books. And for other information, screen-based communications on computer – with moving images, sound and interactive graphics – are beginning to replace or accompany print.

The replacement of longer written and spoken forms by "soundbites" of (at best) condensed or deconstructed thought, poses serious questions for the nature of typography and the messages it holds. Fractured gobbets of information do not provide the same opportunity for rational exposition that strictly linear text delivers. Instead, they deliver the suggestion of multiple viewpoints, of doubt and revision and change. Of the mutable instead of the immutable. They invite us to question, and do not erect large edifices of thought for our clarification or admiration. So will beauty, order, legibility – and other big value systems – continue to have the same significance? What we want to do with type, how we want to read it and what we read, helps shape the individual characters.

But we also need to examine the origins of the technologies, rather than the aesthetics, for the values in our presentation of the written word to become more apparent. In these pages we give some introduction and comment on the technologies as well as the aesthetics, as well as the media. And we note some of the people. But for each of the heroes, or the familiar pieces of work, we could find a mass of production and people... it is that which makes any movement significant. Where once typography was a hand-crafted process, tied in specifically with the realization of words on paper, now type exists in the same medium (digital code) as images and sounds. What makes it distinct is, perhaps, the engine under which it works, through which it becomes typography. The engine has been rebuilt and reinvented at several stages over the past century or so.

Nineteenth-century public speaking often featured speeches of several hours. These were delivered with the complex sentence structure familiar from written communication of the time, sub-clauses stacked within clauses, working towards the careful (if not laboured) presentation of a rational argument. Today our public speaking takes its lead from the soundbite culture of the television, with the emotional "truth" being a more popular element of communication than any pretence of reason. The more ephemeral media of popular press, television and internet pages is of greater influence than any fine printing or tastefully produced broadcast. More than a billion people can see Rupert Murdoch's Star television stations across Asia, covering many languages and scripts. What implications does this have for the nature of typography and of text?

*Remix* tells a story of how words became images. Once words sat in lines, arranged in blocks, sometimes with pictures. At the end of the nineteenth century, the invention of mechanized type composition and casting laid one of the foundation stones for mass-communication, along with the improved reading level of the population. Advances in photography (and its application to half-tone block making for letterpress print) along with improvements in lithography, advanced the potential for printing images. At the end of the twentieth century, rapid advances in computers and screen-based systems of audio-visual and interactive communication have begun to mark a distinctive move from the supremacy of text in mass communication. The growth of global media groupings, and the economics of their product, also have a bearing on the nature of these images.

What follows is a sketch, or sketches, a remix and a dub. It takes its narrative lead from folk tales and its metaphor from contemporary music. *Remix* is not a historical enquiry. That is in the reading list, and in part in the earlier volume. These pages tell some stories, suggest some of the areas of enquiry, intimate through details other events, and weave all this together in a form of typographic plot. But this selection is culled from many tales that could have been told.

Much of the earlier book, *20th-Century Type*, was written on paper in the famous domed reading room of the British Library when it was within the British Museum. Sometimes it would take days to retrieve relevant books from storage. A little of this remix, including this section, was assembled in the new British Library on a portable computer, while most of it was written on the same machine in homes and hotel rooms. We may have lost something in the change, but not the time it can sometimes take to retrieve a book from the library storage. The first book I searched for on the new computerized order system (Theodore Low De Vinne's book of 1900, *Treatise On the Processes Of Type-Making*) was unavailable, marked DESTROYED. Here, with no claim for equal significance, is some kind of replacement. Test to destruction.

Points in time, be they 2000, 2001, 1990, 1900 – or whatever is deemed significant – provoke reflection on the past and the future. As the ancient Greeks pictured it, our notion of the future is of something sneaking up behind us, while the past recedes in front – and so we dream the future with the materials accumulated from our present culture.

The years around 1900 saw anticipation of change and proposals for it, along with some fundamental shifts in the technology of typography. There were intellectual and artistic responses, involving radical visions of how the new century should take shape, along with a yearning for lost values. These dreams – of futures based on the past – projected futures based on fears as much as hopes. These conflicting concerns were the seeds of Modernism – the over-arching name that we give to a movement across many disciplines (from psychoanalysis to architecture) which is central to the story in these pages, too.

A long period of relative peace between the leading nations had helped lay the basis for waves of industrialization and social change. Not far into the new century, it was the outbreak of the First World War in 1914 that finally brought an end to the period of growth and unprecedented riches in the world's most powerful economies. Before that happened, the first fourteen years of the twentieth century allowed the bedding-in of crucial technological change in print and the fomenting of aesthetic issues that were to underlie the coming decades in typographic thought.

Tension between the old and new technology took a number of forms. First there was a looking back at and reviving of lost values and lost modes of expression, a nostalgia that is apparent in the work of the small presses in Britain and the United States and the artist-craft groups such as the Secession movements in Austria and Germany. In contrast, there were new practices derived from the new print methods (notably developments in colour lithography and breakthroughs in machine-set type), and there were also pressures from the changing technologies and mass production. This search for and questioning of "the new" underlay movements such as the *Neue Sachlichkeit*, or "new objectivity", in Germany. Involved in this was a revising of typography, along with a general distinguishing of the significance of design in industrial processes from the earlier embodiment of the design process within craft practices.

The notion of typography was something largely different from the meaning carried today: then typography embraced much that is now within the job description of the printer, or has simply ceased to exist. The printer was the overriding figure, uniting the various processes in manufacturing the printed object, and graphic design had yet to emerge fully as a separate skill. The typesetter was one with the typographer.

The Arts and Crafts Movement in Britain was a key manifestation of craft revivalism that helped spawn an awareness of the space for design. It attacked the low standards of print and the aesthetic it saw as a product of modern industrial culture. William Morris (1834–96) had a

wide influence through his work at the Kelmscott Press in the 1890s. His colleague in that enterprise, Emery Walker, set up the Doves Press in 1900 with Thomas Cobden-Sanderson. Together they designed the one type that the press held, a roman cut in one size only by Edward Prince (who had worked with Morris); like Morris's Golden, Troy and Chaucer faces this was based on a fifteenth-century model from Jenson. Cobden-Sanderson's axiom on typography displays the quest for a functional but interpretative form for the characters, pointing the way towards Modernist thought to come. In it he asserts that the only duty of typography is "to communicate to the imagination, without loss by the way, the thought or image intended to be communicated by the author". The Walker/Cobden-Sanderson face had a brief, but glorious, life: it was used by the Doves Press for the finest of private press books, peaking with the Doves' Bible. However, the matrices came to a violent end when Cobden-Sanderson smashed them and threw the lot into the Thames after a row with Walker – reputedly over who had the better claim to having created the face.

The manner in which the private press books conceived of the various elements of a page as parts of a whole finds a strong echo in the work of the group of artists and designers in Vienna who formed the Secession group (from 1897). Some of them later went on to set up the Wiener Werkstätte (from 1903). The distinctive development of Arts and Crafts and Art Nouveau ideas that this group showed was apparent in the typographic exercises of Koloman Moser. His illustrative calligraphy for the Secession magazine *Ver Sacrum* and his logotypes explored letterforms beyond the rigidity of established foundry faces. Initially his work was florid, organic, Art Nouveau-influenced, but it became more geometric. A masterpiece of the Secession/Wiener Werkstätte's print output is the luxurious commemorative book for the Austro-Hungarian royal print works, produced in 1904, featuring a typeface by Rudolf von Larisch, a title page and initial letters by Moser, and woodcuts by Czeschka. The similarities with Kelmscott work are apparent – the typeface is drawn from fifteenth-century Venetian precedents, and the text is set into wide decorated margins.

In Germany a similar mixing of ideas was present: between notions initially connected with the Art Nouveau style (here, called Jugendstil) moving on to less decorative work. The most distinctive of Art Nouveau typefaces was designed by Otto Eckmann for the Klingspor foundry in 1900; Eckmann was available in two weights, both relatively heavy. It mixed the organic themes of the Jugendstil with the black-letter tradition of Germany, reflecting the medieval pen in the open bowls of letters. It was a distinctive display face, but low on legibility thanks in part to the poor letterforms derived from the overwhelming styling. Producing such sports in metal required considerable investment in time and money, but this perhaps paid off for Klingspor as Eckmann proved to be the definitive Art Nouveau face. Eckmann did not reap much benefit: he died of tuberculosis in 1902, aged 37.

Peter Behrens (1868–1940) is the German designer who travelled furthest in his ideas in this decade. His interests

ECKMANN
Initialen · u · Vignetten

Gesetzlich
geschützt!

Rudhard'sche Gießerei
in Offenbach am Main

Left: from *Schriften und Ornamente*, issued in 1900 by the Klingspor foundry in Germany to promote the release of Otto Eckmann's eponymous type. One of the better known Jugendstil/Art Nouveau faces, the soft forms of its characters are not derived from calligraphy so much as brush-strokes imitative of organic forms, such as plants and trees. Scorned by later generations as too decorative and so consigned to signal a period and style, this face typifies the Art Nouveau reference to Nature, finding in it a quasi-spiritual touchstone for type form. Eckmann was a painter whose career ranged across the applied arts. **p.13** went from type design through to architecture, and could claim credit for helping found the notion of "corporate identity". From mixing traditional German gothic (also called black-letter, or *textur*) type with Jugendstil illustrative work, he moved on to question the ornamental, working to a logic derived from modern industrial methods. Around 1900 his typographic ideas can be seen in the face he designed for Klingspor, Behrens Roman, which like Eckmann's, is a pen-drawn roman but less florid and more related to the German black-letter tradition. At about the same time, Behrens designed a book set in sans serif: Feste des Lebens was an abrupt break with the expected gothic of the *textur* variety, but can be seen as a precursor of the German evolution from black-letter to a reliance on bold sans serifs. Behrens's most

famous work came in 1907 when he was commissioned to review the visual identity of AEG. It is a large multinational today, and still has an identity derived from the logotype of Behrens. From the graphic identity and how this should be applied, Behrens's work progressed through the products to buildings: the turbine factory of 1909 represented a seminal development in architecture in its extensive use of glass. His approach indicates how typography goes well beyond concerns about legibility/readability; it illustrates a wider purpose for typeface character.

The German interest in sans serif, as a modern development from the custom of heavy black-letter, was reflected elsewhere with a search for a sans face of the era, rather

Above: the Wiener Werkstätte logo, which was probably designed by Koloman Moser, 1903, inverts a typographic mark Moser originally used to denote the two Ms in a title on a bookbinding he made in 1896.
Left: in 1905 a booklet was published carrying the marks of WW artists and craftsmen. Here, from top: Friedrich König, Adolf Böhm and Gustav Klimt.
Far left: design by Adalb Carl Fischl, 1900, rationalizes the alphabet forms within a set of angles and curves, but in the process loses legibility as the distinction between characters becomes seriously eroded.

than the numerous and largely undistinguished cuts amassed during the nineteenth century. The American Type Founders' (ATF) amalgamation of firms had about fifty "gothics" in its early specimen book, covering everything from extra-condensed to extra-extended. Yet one of the first faces Morris Fuller Benton (1872–1948) was asked to develop as their chief designer was a new sans. This drew on tradition, and on new market demand, as the face was targeted at the burgeoning requirements of advertising. Benton's drawings in 1902 amalgamated the qualities of the early nineteenth-century models: the resulting Franklin Gothic stands out in contrast to Stempel's Akzidenz Gothic of 1896 (another gothic destined to last throughout the twentieth century) by breaking from any regular line. Details such as the thinning of strokes where rounds join stems give a life to the

face that distinguishes it from other heavy sans. It was released in 1905 and proved popular, with Benton cutting further weights besides the initial extra bold. Pushing out the whole family of ATF gothic faces (Alternate Gothic and News Gothic being just two other weight variants) was an early example of the type foundries' latching on to the printer's requirement for a full range of weights and sizes in one face, rather than odd sizes and weights of dramatically different cuts.

A different gothic was being drawn by the other prolific type designer of the period – Copperplate Gothic by Frederic Goudy (1865–1947), also for ATF. This, in fact, is not a gothic at all, in the sense of being either a bold sans face or a black-letter face (the word "gothic" in type description is

Franklin Gothic *24pt*

# ABCDEFGHIJKLMN
# OPQRSTUVWXYZ
# abcdefghijklmn
# opqrstuvwxyz

News Gothic *24pt*

ABCDEFGHIJKLMNOPQRSTUVWXYZ
abcdefghijklmnopqrstuvwxyz

applied to so many kinds of faces that it is all but useless). Instead it is a face that owes its reference to the forms of letters chiselled in stone, which are described as glyphic. Copperplate Gothic crosses boundaries: the serifs are so tiny as to be almost invisible in small sizes, merely helping hold the definition of character and converting the appearance to that of a sharp sans. The appearance is stylized, and the face was intended – and is still used – for titling and cards. It has found use in packaging, combining a crisp legibility with character. There is a subtle inflection of stroke weight – note the capital "C" – giving a dynamic that is missing with constant line sans serifs.

The type design and typographic development of this period took place against the gradual acceptance of the crucial role

Opposite: Morris Fuller Benton's Franklin Gothic (drawings from 1902, released 1905) and News Gothic (1908) were among many faces he designed for American Type Founders. These aimed to serve the fast-growing demand for display advertising type. They draw on the handcut character of nineteenth-century wood letter, retaining a sense of individual, lively calligraphic form at the expense of geometric unity.
Right: Cheltenham, created by Bertram Goodhue in 1896, was a popular display type, remarkable not for any beauty, but for robustness and flexibility, being cut in many weights and sizes.

# KING
## OF ALL TYPE

The Cheltenham Family

The sovereignty of the Cheltenhams in the big world of advertising has been thoroughly established. The growing popularity of the new members which have recently been added is an indication that this most pleasing type family will remain in favor for many years to come. When we consider the versatility and dignity of this monarch of display, we readily appreciate the reason for its phenomenal success. The progressive printers and publishers buying liberal weight fonts are certain to give the Cheltenhams first place in their composing rooms. Never in the history of type casting has the printing trade been presented with such variety and harmony in a single series of type faces. Its intrinsic worth and great adaptability is acknowledged by all. Sold in weight fonts at our regular body type prices that hot-metal setting would come to play. At the end of the nineteenth century the launching of mechanized typesetting with the hot-metal machines of Linotype (1886) and Monotype in the 1890s formed the basis for the massive expansion in printed production, enabling much greater productivity in setting. These machines required their own proprietary faces to be cut for the matrices from which the hot-metal letters would be formed (as lines of type with Linotype, or as individual characters with Monotype; hence the names). While the Linotype had been enthusiastically received for the mass printing of newspapers and magazines (six thousand machines in place by 1900), the Monotype machine was now emerging as a genuine rival, offering qualities that could compare with cold-metal handcrafted typesetting. In 1905 the Monotype caster was improved to cope with larger sizes – casting up to 24 point, albeit only able to compose up to 12 point. In 1907 Monotype developed with a faster keyboard, copying the typewriter layout, with extra keys.

Alongside this technology push, there were moves to make consistent standards in measurement. In America and Britain agreement was reached on the point system, though continental Europe still worked to a different measure, which made for some difficulties in the compatibility of faces and equipment. Although the points system was first proposed by Fournier in Paris in 1737, and later amended by Didot to a measurement of one point equalling 0.3759mm, it was only

in 1886 that American foundries settled on a point size of 0.3515mm.

Despite its lack of decimal logic, the system often still applies, overlapping with metric and imperial measurements, and is a testament to industrial inertia. And that is a force at times as powerful as the revolutionary urges more typically covered in these pages.

**Copperplate** *24pt*

# A B C D E F G H I J K L M N
# O P Q R S T U V W X Y Z

Opposite: the American Type Founders Company, formed in 1892 from the merger of many type foundries, came to dominate the American type market with its breadth of choice, supported by strong marketing. Its substantial and durable catalogues not only demonstrated the fonts in the graphic styles of the day, but did so in a way that showed the variety of expression possible with a large family of cuts. This encouraged printers to consider buying different weights and sizes. Here News Gothic is put through its paces.
Left: Copperplate Gothic, designed in 1901 by Frederic Goudy and released by ATF, was not rated by its designer and indeed is a curious amalgam of traditions. It draws on stone-cut lettering in its technique of minute serifs, but lacks the appeal of glyphic precedents. However, the face is seen the world over in titles and cards because of the illusion of crisp form it delivers in small sizes through the near-invisible serifs.

# 1910

# All a poet can do today is warn.

Wilfred Owen 1893-1918

"...we have entered upon a period of revolution which may last fifty years before the revolution is at last victorious in all Europe and finally all the world."

So the Russian Communist theoretician and economist Nikolai Bukharin commented in 1919 to the English writer Arthur Ransome. He was to be executed in 1938 as part of Stalin's purges of likely opposition. Ransome became a great author of children's books. And the political revolution they discussed? Perhaps that ended at various points: with the death of Lenin, the rise of Stalin, or gradually with each of the party bosses who stretched from the 1950s until Gorbachov and Yeltsin finally pulled the plug on Communist Russia in the 1980s and 1990s. But the age of revolution and its results remains.

By the time of the Great War and the Russian Revolution, the notion of revolution could no longer be an isolated explosion, as in the late eighteenth and nineteenth centuries. Communications of telegraph and press and (soon) radio, along with growing mass literacy, saw to the rapid and popular dissemination of dramatic news. The revolution in society brought about by the Great War, 1914–18, its reshaping and fracturing of countries and their societies, left marks that have never disappeared. We only have to look to Sarajevo: 1914 remixed in 1992–6.

But Bukharin's comment does not have to be read with any sense of irony about the subsequent tragic turns of history if matched against the revolution of the graphic arts that came to prominence in this decade.

Cubism and Futurism sprang to prominence, Suprematism and Constructivism extended the aesthetic revolution into pure abstractions, and in general "the isms of art" clocked up at a rapid rate. These idealist expressions of the changing times have continued to live with us since. Their effect was to challenge the ground rules of graphic production and design thinking, and whether embraced or reacted against they have helped define not just Modernism but the quest for a sense of what it is to be modern, working in art or communication in the twentieth century. That revolution took fifty years or less to impact on every city in the world. Bukharin, editor of both key Communist newspapers *Pravda* and *Izvestia* at various times, may have accepted his prediction as being accurate at least in its recognition of the internationalism and power of media.

By 1910 there were profound challenges across Europe to the assumptions about vision and language. This is most famously recognized in fine art with Cubism's violent fracturing of realism. The Cubism of Braque and Picasso compressed and analysed the planes involved in presenting three-dimensional forms, bringing in the fourth dimension of time to add to space. Objects could be viewed from more than one perspective in a single image. In their experiments with *papiers collés* montage constructions in 1911 and 1912 they introduced the sense of popular print and the abstraction of typographic communication into their work. The Italian Futurist painters Balla, Carra and Severini responded to this

by also drawing on typographic materials, incorporating newspapers and other print into their work. The Futurist manifesto called for the expression of the dynamic forces at work in society, and the populism and ephemeral nature of mass-print was a daily manifestation of this energy.

The Futurist mission to question and shock was led by the writings and work of Filippo Tommaso Marinetti (1876–1944). Marinetti advocated the principle of "words-in-freedom". He challenged the need for orthodox language, both in its verbal and visual contexts. In his 1914 book *Zang Tumb Tumb* the idea found fresh typographic form, with stories/poems as visual/verbal exercises, doing with type what the Futurist artists were attempting in paint, collage and sculpture.

The basis for this work can be read in Marinetti's 1913 manifesto *Destruction of Syntax – Imagination without Strings – Words – Freedom*. Here he fires a verbal flame-thrower at Italian cultural history and then promises to set off his own fireworks to give a new force to the word:

"I initiate a typographic revolution aimed at the bestial nauseating idea of the book of passéist and D'Annunzian verse, on seventeenth-century handmade paper bordered with helmets, Minervas, Apollos, elaborate red initials, vegetables, mythological missal ribbons, epigraphs and Roman numerals. The book must be the Futurist expression of our Futurist thought. Not only that. My revolution is aimed at the so-called typographical harmony of the page, which is contrary to the ebb and flow, the leaps and bursts of style that run through the page. On the same page, therefore, we will use three or four colours of ink, or even twenty different typefaces if necessary. For example: italics for a series of similar or swift sensations, bold face for the violent onomatopoeias, and so on. With this typographical revolution and this multicoloured variety in the letters I mean to redouble the expressive force of words."[1]

Elsewhere Marinetti set down his notion of typography for the emerging medium of cinema.

"Filmed words-in-freedom in movement (synoptic tables of lyric values – dramas of humanised or animated letters – orthographic dramas – typographical dramas – geometric dramas – numeric sensibility, etc.)."[2]

Such clattering of words together is the equivalent of the conflicting, disintegrated elements within Futurist paintings, and of the discordant "music" performed by Marinetti, Soffici and Carlo Carra (1881–1966). The magazine *Lacerba* published a series of Carra's free-word experiments in 1914, "Tipografia in liberta", propagandizing a sense of purely expressive, unstructured typography that perhaps had to wait until the digital age for its full realization. The "dynamism" it sought to represent was that of the new industrial age, but it was not a dynamism that found easy accommodation in the fledgling mechanized type technology of the era. Instead, the long-standing craft of handsetting was still required to realize such free-word pieces: the machine-age aesthetic only found its individual form through handcrafting.

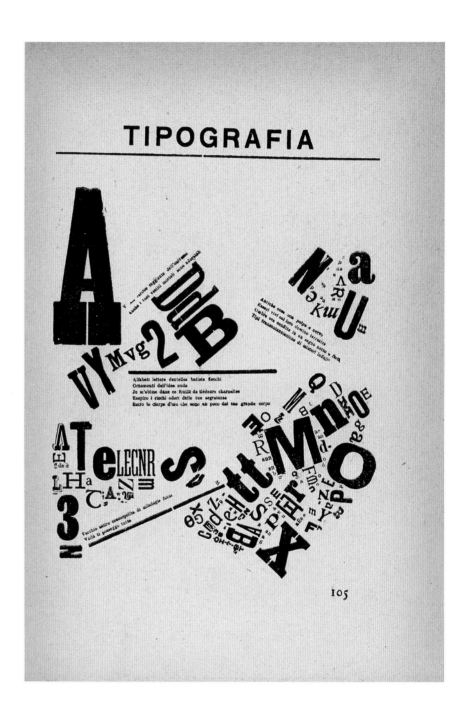

Previous page: *Manifestazione interventista* by Carlo Carra, 1914, a collage of paper and paint on board. The Italian Futurist painter explores the Futurist principles of dynamism, speed and conflict with techniques that put words into motion by using layers, rotation, and violent juxtaposition of elements to break free of both pictorial and text conventions. Above: war loans poster by Lucien Bernhard, 1915. This exemplifies the brutal simplicity of the German Plakatstil. Strong colours, one image, the advertiser's name, and a call-to-action copyline – ad rules that would become commonplace later.

Opposite right: page from *BIF & ZF + 18* by Ardengo Soffici, 1915, a book of typographical experiments using found and constructed imagery that aimed to reinvent literary communication. Soffici (1879–1964) was a painter and writer who had broken with the Italian Futurist group by this point. Below: cover and inside page of the novel *Zang Tumb Tumb*, 1914, by Filippo Marinetti. The Futurist leader explores his idea of "words-in-freedom" by taking a true story of an incident in the Balkan war of 1912 and telling it through free-form layouts that are full of typographic puns and word-plays, and challenge the linearity of reading.

The Russian Futurists were substantially different from the Italian Futurists, having different roots and different results, but they were no less influential. They took inspiration from the Cubist break with representational traditions, but were unconnected with the Italian manifestos. Instead, their reaction was against Russian symbolist art and sought to revive some primitive forms as a rejection of Czarist culture. Between 1912 and 1916 the various artists loosely grouped under this banner combined to produce work that included several innovative books and other printed artefacts.

In what might seem a conundrum given our subject, these books are often distinguished by an absence of typography. Lithographic, with the artist's calligraphy as well as images, in effect they "painted" the page of the book, removing the need for typographical input and its restrictions. The adventures of design discovered in the free form given to the poster by lithography were extended into book form. The 1912 *Worldbackwards* and 1913 *Explodity* by Alexei Kruchenykh also used techniques such as rubber stamp blocks to print poems, accompanied by stencilling or potato-printing of key letters. Such Futurism seemed to be going in the opposite direction to the Italian movement, rejecting rather than embracing modern processes.

The most influential of Russian Futurist books did feature type. Vladimir Mayakovsky's *A Tragedy* varies type weight, has incongruous upper case and displays a dramatic use of white space to construct a visual metaphor for the emotive response sought from Mayakovksy's play. It was designed by Vladimir and David Burliuk, and includes their drawings. Thought to have been admired by Alexander Rodchenko (1891–1956) and El Lissitsky (1890–1941), the book can be seen as an antecedent of postwar, post-Revolution graphics.

Out of the Russian Futurists evolved other significant movements which were to probe the boundaries of typography further. Kasimir Malevich's Suprematist paintings from 1916, boldly non-figurative and geometric, provoked thought about the two-dimensional plane and its formal arrangements. This had a direct impact on El Lissitsky who found a link with typographic communication: his early Constructivist painting of 1919, *Beat the whites with the red wedge*, can be seen in direct connection with his children's story book *Of Two Squares* (conceived in 1920, published 1922), which explores typographic construction and its notions of narrative largely without conventional typographic elements.

Another passing influence on El Lissitsky (a nodal point in typography, whose own work and thought was to be so influential in the 1920s), was that of the English Vorticist movement, another Cubist/Futurist group. The propagandist periodical *Blast*, launched and designed in 1914 by the Vorticist leader Percy Wyndham Lewis (1882–1957), was seen as a direct precedent for Burliuk and Mayakovsky's 1915 publication *Vzyal: baraban futuristov [Took: a futurist's drum]*, which like *Blast* featured a single declamatory word coarsely printed on the cover.

Following a separate path of typographic exploration were the Dadaists, who first appeared around the middle of the First World War in Zurich and then spread to German cities, and to Moscow and Paris. The poetry of Hugo Ball mixed typefaces in a deliberately illogical, nonsensical manner that parodied poetic form. His statement that "the word and the image are one" expresses this desire for a medium free of the mechanical and cultural constraints that beset print. Another key Dadaist, Kurt Schwitters (1887–1948), explored the textural and ironic implications of using printed ephemera. As early as 1919, in his series of works entitled *Merz*, he presented art culled from assorted, perhaps random, typographic communications. In 1919 Raoul Haussmann edited the first issue of the periodical *Der Dada*, with an expressive type cover that extended Futurist experiments. Haussmann, Hannah Hoech and (most notably) John Heartfield pioneered photomontage from 1917, a distinctive Dadaist questioning of the relationship between the representation of surface and space, two and three dimensions.

In Holland this decade saw the birth of the De Stijl movement, formed around the publication of the magazine *De Stijl* in 1917 by the painter, designer and writer Theo van Doesburg (1883–1931). The first cover sported a logotype based on a painting by Vilmos Huszár (1884–1960), which drew the characters in combinations of rectangles – an intimation of the mechanized and electronic signage typefaces used later in the century, as well as a theoretical statement about purity and reduction in form.

While the pioneers of Cubism, Picasso and Braque, did not directly link their art to communication art and typography, the French poet and critic and champion of the Cubists, Guillaume Apollinaire (1880–1918), made an influential connection between the new approach to art and the visual potential of words. He wrote calligrams – poems that used the type and layout of the page as an expressive element of the piece. There are precedents for this, notably Lewis Carroll's dwindling mouse tale/tail sentence and typographic pun in *Alice's Adventures In Wonderland* (1865) or Stéphane Mallarmé's layouts in *Un Coup de Des* (1897). They are part of an ongoing stream of literary self-consciousness with visual play that can be traced back at least as far as Laurence Sterne's wit-laden *Tristram Shandy* (1760). Another French writer experimenting with form around the time of Apollinaire was Blaise Cendrars; his 1913 "simultaneous" book *La Prose du Transsiberien et de la petite Jehanne de France* was a two-metre long poem, printed in different colours and type sizes. He dispensed with the neutral page background by having the poem printed over an abstract painting specially designed by Sonia Delaunay.

The various movements outlined above had no direct effect on mainstream communications – they were creating art pieces. However, the questions they raised can be seen to feed through to commercial activity within a decade. Their questioning of conservative typographic form, where words on a page were presented either formulaically or in a manner aimed to smooth and please the eye, led them to devise methods that would serve the fast-expanding needs of advertising where the ability to arrest and provoke the eye was vital.

Left: two consecutive spreads from *Le-Dantyu as a Beacon* by Ilya Zdanevich, a drama about art involving two painters and offering multiple readings. It included obscene double meanings. Zdanevich (1894-1975) was a Russian Futurist who from 1910 onwards helped to develop the idea of "zaum" – a theory of "transrational language" that took words and other forms of expression beyond their conventional use. In the play, each spread can have several possible readings. Although Zdanevich began his dramatic works in Tbilisi, Georgia, this volume was not produced in Paris until 1923.

While these revolutionary ideas were filtering through, the world of commercial typography was seeing a concerted effort to improve standards by reviving classic faces or forms. This revivalism is a key theme of the century's typography, with waves of rediscovery adding layers of historical reference to the typographic culture.

The pace of technological change was quickening, particularly with the refinement of typesetting machines. In 1911 the Linotype was developed to carry three magazines of matrices at once, the different fonts interchangeable at the press of a lever. In the same year this was increased to four magazines, and almost annual announcements pushed the technology forward (a forerunner of the technology upgrades familiar with software and hardware today). Linotype's developments were not a result of curiosity but competition. And Monotype was not the only competitor; in 1912 Intertype launched a rival linecasting system following the expiry of the Mergenthaler patent on the basic system. In 1918 the *New York Times* ordered Intertype casters, firmly establishing the company. Headline setting was outside the capabilities of the Linotype and Monotype, still requiring wood-letter. But the launch of the Ludlow machine for casting from hand-assembled large-character matrices pointed the way forward and heralded the decline of the wood-letter industry and its skills in hand-cut letters.

Meanwhile, Monotype was strengthening its grip on fine machine typesetting, with developments including the increase of point size capability to 24 point in 1914. But

BLAST First (from politeness) ENGLAND

CURSE ITS CLIMATE FOR ITS SINS AND INFECTIONS

DISMAL SYMBOL, SET round our bodies,
of effeminate lout within.

VICTORIAN VAMPIRE, the LONDON cloud sucks
the TOWN'S heart.

A 1000 MILE LONG, 2 KILOMETER Deep

BODY OF WATER even, is pushed against us
from the Floridas, TO MAKE US MILD.

OFFICIOUS MOUNTAINS keep back DRASTIC WINDS

SO MUCH VAST MACHINERY TO PRODUCE

THE CURATE of "Eltham"
BRITANNIC ÆSTHETE
WILD NATURE CRANK
DOMESTICATED
                    POLICEMAN
LONDON COLISEUM
  SOCIALIST-PLAYWRIGHT
DALY'S MUSICAL COMEDY
GAIETY CHORUS GIRL
TONKS

# A B B C D E F G H
# I J K L M N O P Q
# R S T U V W X Y Z

From opposite left: "Il Pleut", a calligram by the poet Guillaume Apollinaire, 1918, drew on ancient texts as well as contemporary experiments. The first issue of *Blast*, 1914, edited and designed by Percy Wyndham Lewis. This was the Vorticist bid to free words (with nineteenth-century wood letter). Above is a 1919 alphabet by Theo van Doesburg based on a square of 25 equal parts. Drawn as a font by The Foundry, 1990s.

perhaps the most significant creative development was Monotype's cutting of Imprint in 1913, the first face specifically developed for machine setting. It was named after a new magazine dedicated to typography, and the type design was by the magazine's editors and founders, Gerard Meynell and J.H. Mason, working with F. Ernest Jackson and Edward Johnston. The face had a large x-height, and a thickened and very regular italic, features designed for the robust requirements of machine setting and printing.

The short-lived *Imprint* magazine and the setting up of the American Institute of Graphic Arts in 1914 signified a new awareness of the role of the graphic designer, as separate from the skills of the type compositor and printer. It was

also in this period that the likes of Frederic Goudy and Bruce Rogers (1870–1957) emerged as eminent figures in their field in America, with Rudolf Koch (1876–1934) and Edward Johnston (1872–1934) in Europe. The type designer could now separate from the printer/foundry, albeit needing a commission or outlet for the manufacture of a typeface. Goudy's prolific work for ATF involved a range of loose revivals, remixing various historical sources through his eye and craft, with occasional commercial pressures brought to bear by the manufacturer (for example, the short ascenders in Goudy Old Style of 1914, a compromise sought by ATF).

The combination of immense calligraphic skill and a new typographic sensibility was apparent in the work of Koch

Right: Centaur, designed in 1914 by Bruce Rogers for publications of the Metropolitan Museum in New York, took its name from being the face for Maurice de Guérin's *The Centaur*, published by Montague Press in 1915. A revival of the fifteenth-century Jenson, it has been widely admired but rarely used – perhaps because its prettiness only bears up under fine printing and then impedes easy reading. It was finally fully released by Monotype in 1929, with an italic. Below right: Imprint was described as the first original face for mechanized typesetting. This Monotype face draws on the eighteenth-century Caslon, but has a larger x-height and thickened strokes for durability. Opposite top: Plantin, a 1913 revival from Monotype based on a sixteenth century Dutch master. Opposite: Underground type by Edward Johnston, 1916, still in use (in its New Johnston digital form) on the London underground system. The first Modern sans serif? Consistent line is relieved by varied characteristics such as a diamond over the "i" and "j", and the uneven "t" bar.

Centaur *24pt*

ABCDEFGHIJKL
MNOPQRSTUVWXYZ
abcdefghijklmnop
qrstuvwxyz

Imprint *18pt*

ABCDEFGHIJKLMNOPQRSTUVWXYZ
abcdefghijklmnopqrstuvwxyz

(designer of Frühling and Maximilian in this decade, among others) and Johnston, whose key typographic achievement is the remarkable sans serif he designed for the London Underground in 1916. This broke with Victorian sans serif precedents by applying a strict classical awareness of forms to the letters, involving an integration of geometric thinking that anticipated the work to be produced in the 1920s. In its new digital form, it still exists in use as the identity typeface of the London undenground system. While it has never been openly available, it soon had an influence on other seminal faces, such as Futura and Gill, while Johnston's knowledge of calligraphy was an inspiration to the young Jan Tschichold.

There was a growing awareness of the need to revive the typographic heritage for the new technology. From 1912 the extensive culture of re-making Garamond began, first at the Parisian foundry Deberny & Peignot, and in the years after at all other major foundries. Put together, the faces show cultural similarities, but also remarkable variations. In effect, Garamond was a reference point and aspiration for a range of new cuts, an ideal to be expressed or a label to be exploited rather than a simple act of faithful copying. Such are remixes.

Plantin *18pt*

ABCDEFGHIJKL
MNOPQRSTUVWXYZ
abcdefghijklmnop
qrstuvwxyz

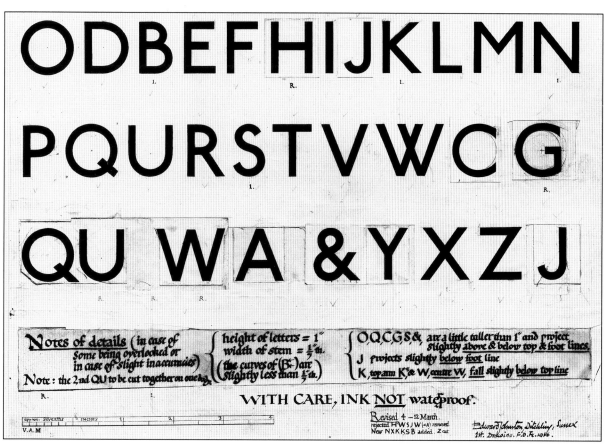

# FUT

URE

The manifestos for much that has happened in graphic design this century were written and visualized in the 1920s. The decade saw a ferment of both radical and conservative typographic ideas. From the experimental came a sense of the Modern, that would soon filter into advertising and other commercial usage; meanwhile, the peaks of typographic history were revived by traditionalists as representing values that needed to be restored. The ideas and activities of these years reveal the emerging significance of typography, its position in the flux of creativity between fine art and architecture, and its value as a crucial political and commercial tool.

At the centre of the emergence of a new typography was the Bauhaus. The work produced by its teachers and students, and by others associated with them or influenced by them, came through a synthesis of the new ideas in art. This radically new school, which taught architecture and the applied arts as interdisciplinary subjects, was founded in Weimar in 1919. Das Staatliches Bauhaus emerged from an earlier, prewar school that had been run by the Belgian architect and designer Henry Van de Velde, renowned for his influential contribution to Art Nouveau. But the agenda of the new school's director, the architect Walter Gropius, a former assistant of Peter Behrens, projected a philosophy that expressed and expanded the emerging Modernist sensibility, in which the integration of art and technology and the development of a mass-production aesthetic were vital. The school's lifespan of 1919 to 1933 mirrored that of the Weimar Republic, and its struggles reflected those of the years – it fought for funds, moved three times in fourteen years and was regularly attacked for its socialist politics.

Typography was not fully a part of the initial Bauhaus programme. The first leader of the Bauhaus's preliminary course, Johannes Itten, included lettering skills and produced some Dada-influenced typographic art of his own, but it was with the arrival in 1923 of László Moholy-Nagy (1895–1946) to run the preliminary course that the Bauhaus began to make a significant statement in graphics; indeed, it helped forge the idea of graphic design studies. His five years at the college produced a body of work and publications that set down ideas that were to spread around the world. This period saw graphic design, photography and film take a more prominent role in the output of the Bauhaus than they had before or would afterwards, a direct result of Moholy-Nagy's teaching. Gropius had set up the school's teaching structure from the viewpoint that architecture was the ultimate objective and thus building was the final course of study, following on from the other applied arts. His successors in the role of director – first Hannes Meyer, in 1928, and then Mies van der Rohe, in 1930 – further emphasized the architectural content of the school programme. However, Gropius reached out from his own architectural background to create a school that made a major contribution to the development of graphics, products, furniture and fine art as well as architecture. Teachers such as Paul Klee, Wassily Kandinsky and Lyonel Feininger in painting, and the outside influences of other artists such as van Doesburg and El Lissitsky, ensured a dramatic and

eclectic contribution to new ideas in two-dimensional communication.

In 1923 Moholy-Nagy called for "absolute clarity in all typographical work". He argued that:

"Communication ought not to labour under preconceived aesthetic notions. Letters should never be squeezed into an arbitrary shape – like a square.... A new typographic language must be created, combining elasticity, variety and a fresh approach to the materials of printing, a language whose logic depends on the appropriate application of the processes of printing."[1]

At the forefront of Moholy-Nagy's graphics output was the Bauhaus books series from 1923. His advertising for the books incorporated Constructivist and De Stijl ideas – the elements of the page such as rules, full points and blocks of text, colour and white space are organized asymmetrically on modular grids (as opposed to traditional centring on linear grids) and are suggestive of the paintings of van Doesburg and Mondrian. The covers, which worked as a series but had different arrangements, stripped down the design to elements that were purely typographic and arranged these so boldly as to be a statement at least as strong as the meaning of the words displayed.

For all its self-consciousness and relationship with ideas in related art movements, this work is among the first examples of a commercially relevant new typography, showing a move from the more strident art statements of Futurist, then Dada, De Stijl and Constructivist typography. More than being idealistic manifestos, the Bauhaus books, and following work from the printshop and advertising course, were a stepping stone into relating these ideas to mass communication.

In his 1925 essay on "Contemporary Typography – Aims, Practice, Criticism", Moholy-Nagy anticipated the replacement of much typographic communication by sound recordings and film images. In response, typography needed to raise itself to a new level of expressive power and effectiveness. This involved embracing and developing the machine age in print production, and moving on from the period of experimental typography that used old technology to express new ideas (which would seem to criticize the Futurists and De Stijl artists) to a more serious grasping of new technology and the new visual experiences of the age. He looked forward to the pages of grey text being transformed into colourful narratives, and being conceived of as a dramatic whole so that individual pages were part of a sequence much like film frames. In this he was a prophet of debates surrounding new media in the 1990s.

In the essay Moholy-Nagy went on to outline principles of new typographic practice. Tension was to be introduced into layouts by contrasting visual elements – such as empty/full, light/dark, multicoloured/grey, vertical/horizontal, upright/oblique – and these were to be achieved chiefly through the disposition of type. Typographic signs were also an element, but not as ornamental borders and the like so

Left: cover of issue number
seven of *Offset Buch und
Werbekunst*, 1926, designed by
Herbert Bayer. The rapid growth
of interest in the work of the
Bauhaus was confirmed by this
printing industry magazine
devoting a special number to it.

**p.35**

beloved of the traditional printshop and typical of the vernacular ephemera.

Moholy-Nagy said there was a need for a standard form of writing, a single design without the two sets of letters involved in lower case and capitals. He lamented the lack of a typeface that had correct proportions, was purely functional and without individual flourish. Attempts at such faces were drawn by Bauhaus students – notably in 1925 by a Bauhaus colleague and former student, Herbert Bayer (1900–85).

Bayer was the first head of a new typography workshop at the Bauhaus, which was established in 1925 when the school moved to Dessau. He held the post until 1928, when he resigned along with Gropius and Moholy-Nagy. As a student he displayed a bold clarity in his work and an integration of the ideas of De Stijl and Constructivist thought. His banknotes for the State of Thuringia, produced in 1923, can be seen as an early signpost of the distinctive Bauhaus look that emerged in graphics. Such a notion of a style dismayed Gropius, who was against the superficial thought implied by the concept of style. But being seen to have a style was inevitable due to the contrast between the new Bauhaus notions of typographic form and those of tradition, particularly the conservatism of German printing with its emphasis on dense black-letter.

Bayer's minimalist sans serif face was one of a number of proposals for such a reductive typeface – others included van Doesburg's alphabet of 1919 and Tschichold's universal

**Albers** *24pt*

lettering a few years later – but it had the benefit of being preached through the Bauhaus course. The argument for a single alphabet was based on the fact that the upper case is not heard, but is only seen. It made written language and its presentation more complex and expensive, demanded more effort in the learning and then in the setting as well as the typesetter's carrying of more characters. Bauhaus publications began dropping the use of capitals from this time. Bayer's single alphabet proposal is distinctive for generating its forms from a declared reductive range of a few angles, arcs and selected lines. This results in a simplicity in which the "m" and "w" are the same inverted, and the "x" is little more than an "o" cut in half and turned inside-out. Bayer developed a number of experimental typefaces in the period 1925–27, mostly of interest only for display purposes, such

as a semi-abstract shadow typeface in which the shadow was all that was left, all the initial outline being removed as unnecessary to the suggestion of the form. His type design ideas finally emerged into the harsh light of commercial availability as Bayer-type for Berthold in 1935, but it was notably conservative, a condensed didone with short descenders and a rather fussy character, a long way from the ideas pioneered at the Bauhaus.

For all the Bauhaus' aspirations to a machine-age aesthetic, the printing workshop under Bayer was restricted pretty much to the old technology of hand-setting. (This provides a neat paradigm for the work of Modernist architects of the period who sometimes simulated the plasticity of concrete, steel and glass forms by rendering over brick or stone.) A

**Bayer** *48pt*

abcdefghijk
lmnopqrstu
vwxyz

Opposite: 1925 design for stencil lettering by Josef Albers (1888-1976), who taught at the Bauhaus from 1923 until it closed in 1933. Albers reduced his alphabet to geometric shapes drawn out of a grid, with the square, the triangle and the circle as the elements (plus the double line for a crossbar). Below the original drawing is a 1990s digital version from The Foundry.
Left: design for a single alphabet by Herbert Bayer, 1925. The geometric reduction of form here sees a consistent arc become a dominant element of characters. Only the "T" is retained from distinct upper-case letterforms.

**p.37**

sans serif face existed in a number of sizes for hand-setting, which could be printed on a platen (flat-bed) press or a rotary proof press. All the printed materials needed by the college – forms, brochures and posters – came from the print department, produced to designs by Bayer or students.

Bayer's teaching was not formal; instead he directed the work of students on real commissions that were pulled into the department. Advertising was of particular interest to Bayer and he promoted ideas on the psychology of advertising and its relationship to the consciousness. The importance of placing arresting and symbolic elements into typographic form was made apparent. The primacy of red and black in two-colour printing, the power of dynamic white space (rather than static borders), highly contrasted type sizes used to express relative values of information and the growing use of photomontage and collage elements were all recognized as key concepts. Bayer's determination that work should contribute to a mass-production age meant that he had all work carried out to standard DIN (German standards authority) sizes of paper.

Bayer was succeeded in 1928 by Joost Schmidt (1893–1948), under whom the printing workshop changed its name to the advertising workshop, revealing how significant this new discipline was to the Bauhaus – it was not possible to train elsewhere in advertising. There was even more emphasis on bringing in outside projects, and Schmidt pushed the Bayer/Moholy-Nagy line – investigating ideas of incorporating photography and the power of high contrast

elements in form and colour. Schmidt encouraged a slightly wider range of typefaces and evolved grids that moved away from the strictly modular, experimenting more with overlaying one simple pattern on another to create dynamic complexities. In Schmidt's time typography became more strongly a part of the Bauhaus core curriculum, being taught over two terms of the preliminary course.

Prior to the Bauhaus becoming typographically energetic, and during its main period of activity in this area (1923–30), there were significant contributions to Modernist graphic communication in the Soviet Union, Holland, elsewhere in Germany, in Poland, Czechoslovakia and Hungary. In the recently established Soviet Union, a whole cluster of artists were exploring new ideas about photomontage and type

Opposite: cover and sample spread from *Of Two Squares* by El Lissitsky, typographical "paintings" constructed in 1920 and printed as a 24-page book in 1922. These Suprematist works, Prouns, were produced in a period in which Lissitsky taught with Kazimir Malevich at the Vitebsk art school, where they launched a radical programme in 1919, renaming the institution Unovis as they propounded Suprematist ideals that unified Cubist and Futurist thinking. The book takes Malevich's idea of the square as the generator of form, presenting a child's story of two squares coming to earth and colliding with black shapes. The red, of course, is triumphant.
Left: cover of *Die Kunstismus [The Isms Of Art]* by El Lissitsky and Hans Arp, 1925. An attempt to summarize the art movements of 1914-24, the book is an interesting artwork in its own right. Lissitsky's layout is locked to a reductive grid of three columns per page, one for each of the three languages used. Akzidenz Grotesk bold, with minimal size variation, is used.　**p.39**

elements in the development of political and commercial design in the 1920s. Chief among them were Lissitsky and Rodchenko.

Lissitsky influenced Moholy-Nagy and van Doesburg, whom he met regularly in the early 1920s. His work varies between the locked-up elements packed into the pages of *The Isms of Art* of 1925 and the light, spare statements involved in his design for Mayakovsky's poems *For Reading Out Loud* in 1923 or Lissitsky's own *Of Two Squares*, his 1920 Suprematist children's story book that explores the relationship between the fourth dimension – time – the three dimensions of the book and the two dimensions of the page. Lissitsky's ideas partly evolved and were propagated through innovative Soviet art schools (Vkhutemas and Vitebsk) where

he was brought in by Kandinsky and Chagall. Here the crossover of innovative ideas in graphic design and the fine art world was at its most fluid, with questions relating to colour, abstraction, form and space being applicable to both, as was the discussion of the social relevance of such debate. The new typographic and illustrative forms that were derived from this teaching can be seen in the poster culture of Moscow in the 1920s.

Rodchenko pushed the integration of photography and type: his mastery of both elements gives his posters a powerful, direct quality. His originality in photography was combined with a sensitivity to the point of focus on type: confrontational slabs of type, with colour integrating word and image, challenge the viewer to find connections and interpret

Opposite: two spreads from *For Reading Out Loud*, a collection of poems by Vladimir Mayakovsky, designed by El Lissitsky and published in Berlin in 1923. Each spread is a poem, and the die-cut tabs help the reader recognize where each one is located, being in alphabetical order with a symbol linking to the page content. Only materials readily available at the typesetter were used, thus illustrations such as the ship and even the inclusion of large characters required rules and bars and other devices to be employed. Besides the constructions, the dynamic white space also stood out.
Right: advertisement for GUM, Moscow's state department store, designed by Aleksandr Rodchenko with text by Mayakovsky, 1923. This Constructivist image is built from blocks of type and product shots to make a figure that says Mozer are the only watches worth having, to be found at GUM.

documentary stories between pictures or typographic elements.

De Stijl and Dada continued to evolve in the 1920s. Theo van Doesburg, a seminal figure in both movements, lived in Weimar between 1921 and 1923 and conducted lectures attended mostly by Bauhaus students. He saw his lectures as a directly subversive element to be spread among the students and to take root within Gropius's system. In 1922 he published the first issue of *Mecano*, a Dadaist journal. Its eclectic mix of elements contrasts with the purer form of the De Stijl magazine that he brought out and which can be seen, along with Lissitsky's work, as the clearest influence on Moholy-Nagy's ideas at the Bauhaus. Like Lissitsky and then Moholy-Nagy, van Doesburg was among the first to be

concerned with creating a new plasticity in print. They all sensed the potential of new technology and the significance of film and broadcast communication.

Kurt Schwitters was close to Lissitsky and van Doesburg in the early 1920s, his work presenting a different synthesis of Dada, De Stijl and Constructivism. His *Merz* assemblages from 1919 evolved into a journal of the same name that ran from 1923 until 1932. Issues featured contributions from influential figures from these movements, including an edition in 1924 that was jointly edited with Lissitsky and a later edition devoted to advertising typography. There is more humour in Schwitters's work than in that of his contemporaries; form and spatial ideas drawn from Lissitsky are mixed with the Dadaist sense of experimentation for disruption's sake. Underlying Schwitters's designs there seems to be a sense of the dislocation required in effective poster and cover art, akin to the "defamiliarization" espoused by Russian Formalist literary theoretician Viktor Shklovsky as a central element of the emerging Modernist consciousness of art. Schwitters's methods, such as laying type over the bold rules that establish the grid, interrupting blocks with other lines or inserting pictures in seemingly unbalanced asymmetrical layouts pick up the ideas of a new typography and begin to disrupt them in a way similar to what had been done with the traditional forms.

Another innovator, working largely in isolation from the seed beds of change, was the printer-typographer Hendrik Werkman (1882–1945). After becoming aware of the new art

Opposite: *Small Dada Evening*, a poster by Theo van Doesburg and Kurt Schwitters, 1922. Hand-lettering with dramatic contrasts of size and weight, mixed with type, and with printer's marks (the hand, the border), may seem anarchistic, but involves the origin of new rules – the diagonal is used as a dynamic, tension-making device, the lettering blocks against the headlines and the red DADA provide a clear hierarchy of typographic communication. Left: Kurt Schwitters' single alphabet of 1927 tried to link sounds closer to forms. He played with heavier forms for vowels, and different versions. The full alphabet here is a 1990s digital recut produced by The Foundry, with variants. Bottom: *Merz 8/9* magazine cover by Schwitters, 1924.

# MeJ STER

Schwitters *28pt*

## ARbCdEeFGhIJKLMNOOPQRSSTUÜVWXYYZ

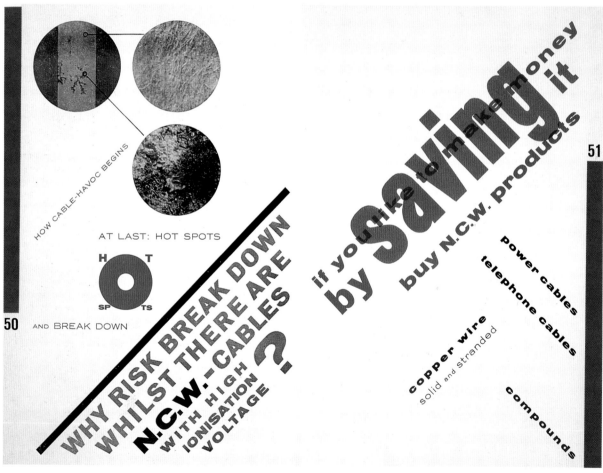

HOW CABLE-HAVOC BEGINS

AT LAST: HOT SPOTS

H O T
O
SP TS

AND BREAK DOWN

WHY RISK BREAK DOWN WHILST THERE ARE N.C.W.-CABLES WITH HIGH IONISATION VOLTAGE?

if you like to make money by **saving** it buy N.C.W. products

**power cables**

**telephone cables**

**copper wire**
solid and stranded

**compounds**

of the early 1920s, he produced, from 1923, his own magazine, *The Next Call*. By 1926 there were nine issues of the magazine, which became increasingly experimental in its investigation of the nature of the printing task. Elements of the printing process – the ink, the paper, the pressure, the wooden or metal types and the pieces of page furniture inserted to hold a chase together, along with colour and form – were all revealed in different ways. Random elements crept into the designs that reflected aspects of the materials and construction of the page. The first issue, for example, included an apparently abstract image that was part of a lock incorporated into the design.

Piet Zwart (1885–1977) was another Dutchman who contributed to the emerging Modernist typography. From an architectural background, his first typographic exercises, around 1920 and 1921, were influenced by the De Stijl group, but by 1925 typography was his main occupation and he developed a strong individual approach. He was prolific in producing advertising and other promotional literature, his designs displaying the most dramatic contrasts in type size possible within the confines of the poster sizes. Characters were used so large as to become abstract forms on the page, as well as existing within words. He often wrote his own copy, which helped with the clever play of words and image. The primary colours red, blue and yellow (also beloved by the Bauhaus) were often used, and in the late 1920s he incorporated more photography, exploring negative images, overprinting and sharp cropping in highly formalized shapes (often a circle, as if a telescopic image). He said that

Tschichold *44pt*

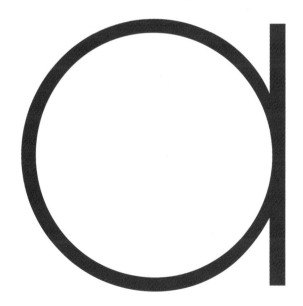

abcdɛfghijklmN
opqrstuvwxyz

Opposite top: on the left, "The Cylinder Press", 1925, and on the right, cover of the first issue of *The Next Call*, 1923, both by Hendrik Werkman, the Dutch printer whose typographic compositions used letterpress elements and other materials – the unusual shape on *The Next Call* is part of a lock. Werkman's pieces deconstructed print, placing the paper on the bed of the press and pressing type and other objects on to it, rather than running paper through a press. Opposite below: spread from a catalogue for the Netherlands Cable Works, designed by Piet Zwart, 1927-8. From 1925 Zwart worked for the client, producing hundreds of pieces that brought the new typography into commercial practice: the dramatic diagonal, the white space, the abstract forms and extreme contrast of type size are typical of this breakthrough work. Left: the universal alphabet was a regular subject of discussion, and Jan Tschichold made his attempt with a 1929 proposal that drew on Bayer's earlier work. A 1990s cut by The Foundry gives the full character set here. **p.45** the simpler and more geometric the character, the more useful he found it.

These various experiments and implementations of a new sensibility in graphic communication found their chronicler and apostle in the seminal book *Die Neue Typographie* ("The New Typography"). Its author, Jan Tschichold (1902–74), was a young Austrian teaching typography and lettering in Munich who had been a close observer of the work of Lissitsky and those at the Bauhaus, among others. He was also an uncompromising modern designer in his own right. In 1925 he published his first writings on the subject in a special issue of the journal *Typographische Mitteilungen*, which was given over to his essay, "Elementare Typographie". In this precocious piece Tschichold introduced Lissitsky's work to the readership of practising printers for the first time. The ideas behind asymmetric typography, sans serif typefaces and a limited choice of faces, plus the relationship of type and white space, were put into terms aimed at providing new rules for the printer. His was a familiar attack on the supposedly debased standards of nineteenth-century printing, and it expressed contempt for the grey nature of blocks of text locked up with little for the eye to be excited by, as well as berating the clutter of advertising typography. While he was partly criticizing the traditions, he was also against some of the variation in print forms derived from more exotic choices in typefaces and typographic arrangements used by printers in the 1920s trying to produce new decorative qualities.

## FUTURA Figuren-Verzeichnis

ABCDEFGHIJKLMNO
PQRSTUVWXYZÄÖÜ
abcdefghijklmnopqrſst
uvwxyzäöü ch ck ff fi fl ff ſſ ſi ſl ß

mager 1234567890 &.,-:;·!?'(*†«»§

Auf Wunsch liefern wir Mediäval-Ziffern 1234567890

ABCDEFGHIJKLMNO
PQRSTUVWXYZÄÖÜ
abcdefghijklmnopqrſst
uvwxyzäöü ch ck ff fi fl ff ſſ ſi ſl ß

halbfett 1234567890 &.,-:;·!?'(*†«»§

Auf Wunsch liefern wir Mediäval-Ziffern 1234567890

**ABCDEFGHIJKLMNO
PQRSTUVWXYZÄÖÜ
abcdefghijklmnopq
rſstuvwxyzäöü ch ck
ff fi fl ff ſſ ſi ſl ß
1234567890**

fett **&.,-:;·!?'(*†«»§**

Tschichold's key points were all directed at creating a purer, elementary functionalism in typography. The thesis could be crudely summarized as: asymmetry, sans serif. A few more words and you would tend to get into the more naïve aspects of the book, which would as a whole be later renounced by Tschichold. But in that it clarified coherent themes in the work of the Modernist typographers, this publication was immensely significant. It presented typography as the graphic arrangement of type and choice of type, rather than a broad descriptive term for other more practical aspects of printing.

It was the man who gave Tschichold his teaching job in Munich who created the most emblematic face of the 1920s:

Futura, designed by Paul Renner. Designed for Bauer and issued from 1927, the face can be seen to have antecedents in the Erbar sans, which was released only a few years before and was also highly popular. Futura (its name was an inspired piece of identity) is distinguished from Erbar by characteristics such as the upper-case "Q" with its tail beginning inside the bowl, and the lack of a tail on the lower-case "j". Renner first designed an even more elemental face, almost abstract in parts (an "r" consisted of just a stem and an unattached point floating where the spur should be). In comparison with other earlier sans, distinguishing features are the clear geometric forms, the single storey "a" and open-tail "g". For twenty-five years Futura would be the leading sans serif face, taking a

Promotional material for Futura, which was issued by the Bauer foundry in 1927. This design by Paul Renner drew on the search for a geometric sans that captured the spirit of the new principles, and coming from a commercial foundry it spread rapidly. A set of ornaments, left, were also made available, that encouraged designers and printers to use imaginatively a set of geometric page furniture that was in keeping with the character of the font. Renner's earlier experimental drawings for such a font were revived in the 1990s as Architype Renner by The Foundry. The "g" and the "r" stand out with quirky features that were ironed out by the time Renner came to draw Futura.

Renner *28pt*

ABCDEFGHIJKLMNOPQRSTUVWXYZ
abcdefghijklmnopqrstuvwxyz

prominent role in advertising in its many variations.

Outside Germany and Holland, one of the first implementations of the new typography in commercial practice was seen in Czechoslovakia, where the artists and designers who went under the Devetsil group banner included two influential typographers, Karel Teige and Ladislav Sutnar. The poet and artist Teige wrote his own version of the new principles in an essay, "Modern Type". Its call for dynamic forms that rejected the traditional was embraced by Sutnar (1897–1976), who was a design teacher as well as a publisher's art director. His work in the late 1920s and early 1930s represented another mixture of the ideas of De Stijl, Constructivism and the Bauhaus teachers.

Bold photomontage is placed with pared down type, alongside demonstrations of the play possible with perspective and the use of colour for depth and foregrounding. Sutnar emigrated to the United States in 1939, giving a second lease of life to his influence.

In Poland, the work of Henryk Berlewi (1894–1967) took a different route forward from the Constructivist ideas spread by Lissitsky. His approach to functional communication was to create a "mechanical art" (*Mechano Faktur*), a systemized idea of creativity that reduced typographic work (amongst other things) to a range of functional elements that could be combined together as building elements. It was a rejection of individualism as well as of the traditional forms associated

Ballmer *28pt*

## abcdefghijklmnopqrstuvvwxyzz
## 0123456789

Left: poster from 1928 by the Swiss designer Theo Ballmer (1902-65), which is for an exhibition of industrial standards. Elements of De Stijl are put through a Bauhaus training, and the commitment to a visible grid prefigures the post-war Swiss Style. Note that just two weights of type are used, one for the headline, one for text, all text ranged to a line. The alphabet developed by Ballmer for this and other posters of the period takes the grid also, with forms tending towards the square. Architype Ballmer, top, is a 1990s digitized version by The Foundry. Opposite: poster by Vilmos Huszár (1884-1960), for an exhibition of industrial arts, 1929. This Hungarian, who lived in The Netherlands, contributed to the first issue of *De Stijl* but left the group in 1923. The poster shows his merging of typographic and abstract shapes so that original letterforms, blocks of colour and geometric pattern project a dynamic image that suggests the three-dimensional and figurative without ever being explicit. It straddles a border between the experimental origins of the new typography, and the stylized outcome of the work, Art Deco.

with a past age. Berlewi went on to apply his ideas by establishing an advertising agency as well as promoting them in other areas of the applied arts.

For all this revolution in the creation of a typography that reflected the Modernist sensibility, the mass of printed communication continued to conform to traditional values, for good or bad. And it was dismay at the latter that drove the traditionalists to argue for the restoration of values they felt had been debased in the move to greater mass communication.

Publication of the seventh and final issue of the typographic journal *The Fleuron*, in 1930, is a crucial point in the recording and exploration of traditional typographic values. Over its seven issues, 1500 pages and eight years during the 1920s, *The Fleuron* set out to cover the quest for the highest typographic standards in Europe and the USA. Despite a prestigious list of contributors there was no place in the index for any designer who might have fallen under the description "Modernist".

In the final issue, Stanley Morison, the editor, set out the principles behind the tradition explored in *The Fleuron*. His "First Principles of Typography" addressed the craft of book design in particular, but he commented on innovations in other areas. In his postscript to the final issue he attacked those who sought to work outside his rules:

This page: Fournier ligature. Opposite: Bembo, Baskerville, Fournier and Bodoni were in a wave of refined revivals by the Monotype drawing office in England during the 1920s, guided from 1922 by the advice of arch-traditionalist Stanley Morison. Bembo (1929), like Monotype's Poliphilus (1923) before it, was based on the designs of punchcutter Francesco Griffo, working for the Venetian printer Aldus Manutius (1450-1515). Its sharp serifs are seen as delivering "brightness"; the face remains popular in editorial work. Baskerville (1924) revived the work of eighteenth-century English printer John Baskerville. Bodoni (1921) cleaned up and revived the "modern" face associated with Giambattista Bodoni (1740-1813) of Parma, which had already been recut by the Italian foundry Nebiolo in 1901 and ATF in 1911 – but the most admired revivals were to be those cuts created by Giovanni Mardersteig (1892-1977) for his private press Officina Bodoni from the mid-1920s. Fournier (1925) was a result of Morison's enthusiasm for the light roman of the eighteenth-century French printer Pierre Simon Fournier.

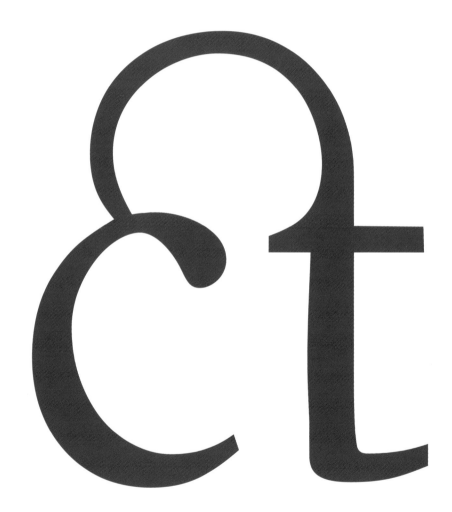

"The apostles of the 'machine age' will be wise to address their disciples in a standard old face – they can flourish their concrete banner in sans serif on title pages and perhaps in a running headline. For the rest, deliberate experiments aside, we are all, whether we like it or not, in absolute dependence upon ocular law and national custom."

In a sense, Morison comes quite close to the Bauhaus search for simple, non-decorative, clear forms of typography in which every element is significant to the communication. But he was a long way away in how he saw such principles being implemented.

"No printer should say 'I am an artist therefore I am not to be dictated to, I will create my own letter forms,' for, in this humble job, individualism is not very helpful. It is no longer possible, as it was in the infancy of the craft, to persuade society into the acceptance of strongly marked and highly individualistic types – because literate society is so much greater in mass and correspondingly slow in movement. The good type designer knows that, for a new fount to be successful, it has to be so good that only very few recognise its novelty." (*From* "First Principles of Typography")

Morison's words set in print what had existed as good practice and what underlay the finest achievements of the print revival projected by the private presses. For the young typographer-compositor in a printworks, and as a text for

**Bembo** *24pt*

ABCDEFGHIJKLMNOPQRSTUVWXYZ
abcdefghijklmnopqrstuvwxyz

**Baskerville** *24pt*

ABCDEFGHIJKLMNOPQRSTUVWXYZ
abcdefghijklmnopqrstuvwxyz

**Fournier** *24pt*

ABCDEFGHIJKLMNOPQRSTUVWXYZ
abcdefghijklmnopqrstuvwxyz

**Bodoni** *24pt*

ABCDEFGHIJKLMNOPQRSTUVWXYZ
abcdefghijklmnopqrstuvwxyz

evening classes to call on, this essay was a valuable marker. Morison addressed his text to the "amateur", even though by being published in *The Fleuron* it was going to the elite (there was a very small, specialized print run – 1000 copies printed on English-made wove, and 210 on English handmade wove paper). In 1936, though, the essay was reprinted in British, American and Dutch editions, and after the Second World War it was translated into German, Danish, Dutch and Spanish, and reprinted again.

A glance through the index of *The Fleuron* shows that there was no room for Bauhaus artists or other Modernists, but the eclectic English craftsmen Edward Johnston and Eric Gill (1882–1940) made it, with a lengthy essay on Gill appearing in the final issue. Gill Sans was Eric Gill's first face to be issued for Monotype, and it quickly became popular, embracing the simple, geometric qualities advocated by the new typography while having a liveliness that displays a sense of the hand behind it and gives some fluidity to the face when seen in continuous text. The face was initially seen as a titling alphabet (it was derived from a bookshop sign painted by Gill), and was in many ways a publicly available variation on Johnston's sans designed for use on the London Underground, from which it was partly derived (Gill had worked with Johnston a little on the earlier face). But it came to be used more than its antecedent thanks to its distribution and to its distinctive character, which also distinguishes it from being just a rolling out of Johnston. Differences to note are the subtle down-curve of the "R", the half-height middle strokes of the "M" that avoid the optical shading noticeable in

Broadway *24pt*

ABCDEFGHI
JKLMNOPQ
RSTUVWXYZ
abcdefghij
klmnopqrst
uvwxyz

some heavy "M"s, and the dropping of the strictly monotone weight of stroke in the lower case.

Work that is often classified under the tag of Art Deco features certain typefaces and a typographic or calligraphic practice that gave a strong flavour to some print of the interwar period, particularly in stylish advertising on posters and in magazines. The Deco style formally centres around the Paris Exposition Internationale des Arts Décoratifs et Industriels Modernes of 1925 and its advocacy of a revival of decorative craft in modern production. However the Deco label is applied to a range of Moderne trends (distinct from Modernist) apparent in all creative areas from architecture to advertising. It had different inflections in different countries, being particularly strong in France, initially, and in America

Opposite: front page of *The New Yorker*, 1925, after its redesign with Irvin as a special headline face, styled around the logo, which has remained essentially unchanged since. In 1991 Gert Wiescher designed FF New Yorker Type, a complete alphabet, which with its slightly imbalanced angularity and contrasting strokes is typical of the Deco styling. This period effect is almost instant with Broadway, shown opposite and with original brochure this page. Designed by Morris Fuller Benton, 1929, for American Type Founders, it merges fat face and lineale type characteristics and has probably appeared on thousands of restaurant and bar promotions since.

later on, and continued into the late 1930s, passing through Jazz Age style to the streamlined look. Graphic artists working in this vein mixed the new approaches of Cubism and post-Cubism with the bold illustrative traditions that had been worked into Art Nouveau and the Plakatstil's development of advertising language. The most noted of the poster artists of this period was A. M. Cassandre (the pseudonym of Adolphe Jean-Marie Mouron, 1901–68). His posters pared down the language of pictorial image and typographic form and then applied the warp of perspectives drawn from the Modernist artists of Cubism and post-Cubism. Out of this approach came his first face, the semi-abstract, highly stylized Bifur, issued in 1929 by Deberny & Peignot. He explained that it was "designed for advertising...designed for a word, a single word, a poster word". It was not ornamental, he stressed, but an attempt to get back to the essential characteristic of individual letters. "If Bifur looks unfamiliar and strange", he argued, "it is not because I have dressed it up eccentrically but because, in the midst of a fully clothed crowd, it is naked." The type specimen book had Cassandre demonstrating how the face could be used in different ways, such as having colour dropped in on the shadow part of the letter.

The Art Deco look spread rapidly in advertising communication, and in the late 1920s and into the 1930s a magazine page of small ads would often contain a variety of fancy Deco faces that are now mostly long disused. One that was widely employed was Broadway, which was designed by Morris Benton, issued by both American Type Founders and

A.M. Cassandre took the ideas of Modernist pioneers into powerful commercial works, which have become among the most treasured commercial graphics of all time (double copyright paid on these images). His ability to merge image and lettering in one powerful pictorial work made Cassandre's posters highly influential. Left: Nord Express (1927) typifies his combination of reductive elements, vignette colour, and visual puns (here the cities lettered on the track map, and the association between the train and the telegraph speed). Cassandre's unique lettering in his posters occasionally spawned extreme typefaces, the first being Bifur for foundry Deberny & Peignot in 1929, its original promotional brochure shown opposite. Bifur reduces characters to the distinguishing core features, and then suggests the rest by shadow lines.

Monotype at the end of the 1920s. The heavy contrast of thick and thin strokes, made even more extreme in an inlined version, may be highly impractical for widespread use, but this made it all the more suitable as an emblematic face for the Deco style.

Much of what is interesting typographically in Art Deco lettering and layouts was not formalized as a foundry face or under any clear rules, such as those set out by Tschichold or Morison. But one influential Art Deco-related publication was A. Tolmer's *Mise en Page*, published in Paris, which set down principles for the advertising designer and printer and had a practical, commercial application that made it more successful than the more substantial theoretical positions of Tschichold and the Bauhaus designers. It emphasized the

need for a clarity and boldness in execution that could give maximum impact to an advertisement. In this it offered a synthesis of the new typography and the old. In a decade, work from pioneers of art theory had become – if not mainstream – certainly widely practised and discussed.

CREAZIONI
TIPOGRAFICHE
DEPERO

1927

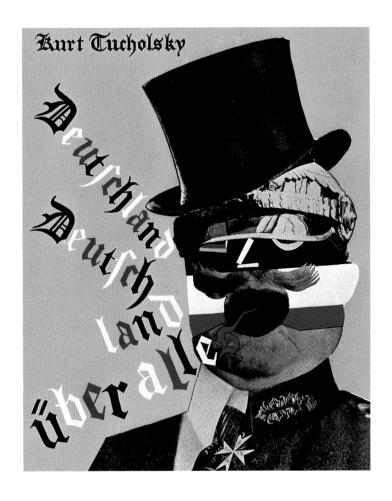

Opposite: design for a visiting card in 1927 by Fortunato Depero (1892-1960). The anarchism and explosiveness of Italian Futurism dissipated in the 1920s, but Depero's application of the ideas in commercial work stands out through his pioneering Campari advertising. Left: book cover designed by John Heartfield, 1929. This pioneer of photomontage sometimes incorporated typography in his pieces in the manner of the work with photography – cutting up and ironically juxtaposing elements, or squeezing meaning out of forms that was never to be seen in the familiar context. Here the black-letter calligraphy is fairly straight, but is deliberately chosen for its association with German nationalism. Some characters are given extra emphasis, drawing them into the image, as with the final "s".

1 9 3 0

TIMES

The decade that endured the Great Depression and ended with the start of the Second World War also saw an increase in international communication and travel. The representation of time and human action – whether through print, cinema or broadcast – moved ever faster and farther. The evolution of a world market, of huge forces at work in controlling demand and supply, gave the collapse in the financial markets the potential for an earth-shattering impact. The international communications and culture could help destabilize nations – and could also be manipulated to help control nations through mass propaganda.

These major themes had their bearing on typographic development. Nowhere more so than in the path taken by the apostle, then apostate, of the new typography, Jan Tschichold. From 1926 until 1933 Tschichold taught and worked in Munich, where he also wrote and published *Die Neue Typographie*. In 1933 he was arrested and removed from his job by the new Nazi government; his ideas were considered *Kulturbolschewismus* ("cultural bolshevism"). The attack was part of the clampdown on all manifestations of Modernism that led to the closure of the Bauhaus in 1933 and the mounting of the Degenerate Art exhibitions, and later to the destruction of modern works of art. Tschichold moved to Switzerland where he taught, and wrote *Typographische Gestaltung*, published in 1935. While still advocating many of the ideas of the earlier work, Tschichold now showed an appreciation for the finesse of classical typography. The title page, with its combination of a swash italic for the author's name, block serif for the title and Bodoni bold for the printer's name, laid out in a balanced composition of symmetrical and asymmetric elements, displays Tschichold's change of heart. The text is also in Bodoni, with block serif headings.

Speaking at a Type Directors' Club seminar in 1959, Tschichold described *Typographische Gestaltung* as "more prudent" than the earlier book:

"... to my astonishment I detected most shocking parallels between the teachings of *Die Neue Typographie* and National Socialism and fascism. Obvious similarities consist in the ruthless restriction of typefaces, a parallel to Goebbels' infamous *gleichshaltung* ('political alignment'), and the more or less militaristic arrangement of lines. Because I did not want to be guilty of spreading the very ideas which had compelled me to leave Germany, I thought over again what a typographer should do. Which typefaces are good and what typefaces are the most practicable? By guiding the compositors of a large Basel printing office, I learned a lot about practicability. Good typography has to be perfectly legible and, as such, the result of intelligent planning. The classical typefaces such as Garamond, Janson, Baskerville and Bell are undoubtedly the most legible. Sans serif is good for certain cases of emphasis, but is used to the point of abuse."[1]

Tschichold's experience of the changed climate of 1930s Germany was, of course, one shared by all who held beliefs not countenanced by the Nazis. The wave of repressive activities that grew in Germany, and later Austria, Holland and France, under the Nazis forced the spread of the ideas pioneered in and around the Bauhaus group of artists and designers. Many went into exile, chiefly to Britain and the United States.

The same was true of Tschichold's adopted homeland of Switzerland, where the first signs of a typographic approach that would influence a whole generation of postwar designers became apparent in the 1930s in the emergence of Swiss Style, later to be called International Style. From the teaching of Ernst Keller (1891–1968) and Alfred Williman at the School of Applied Art in Zurich after the First World War came a practical development of the new modular order expressed in the work of the De Stijl artists and the Constructivists. The establishment of a system for a flexible but firm underlying structure for typographic layouts complements the push to simplify and purify the form of type, as seen in the promotion of new sans serif faces. One student at the Zurich school was Theo Ballmer (1902–65), who went on to study at the Bauhaus. From the late 1920s, he used a visible grid to underpin the typographic order. This anticipates one of the most distinctive ideas associated with the Swiss school of the 1950s and 1960s. The process of deriving the grid and then applying it to order information was a major contribution to the structuring of a typographic designer's work. Ballmer's ideas were mapping out the way ahead. The grid idea, itself, was of course in no way new – a grid underlies the layout of the first book printed with movable type, Gutenberg's 42-line bible of 1452 – but in this era the grid was restated as the bedrock on which typography could be constructed.

Another Swiss student out of the Bauhaus was Max Bill (1908–94). He combined a severity in type choice – Akzidenz Grotesk to the fore – with an approach that created posters that are almost purely typographic and, even then, consist of few words. This was in the tradition of the German Plakatstil artists, given a new twist through Bill's minimalist take on Bauhaus theories. The posters of another leading Swiss designer, Herbert Matter (1907–84), for the clothing company NKZ and then for Swiss tourism, combined an appreciation of the art movements of the time with the development of the typographic craft. All the elements of the image were integrated in one powerful piece, sometimes with no distinct line of type but with the typographic elements worked into the picture.

Matter was one of many designers to go to the United States when it became difficult to work in Europe. Few were under more pressure to leave Germany than those associated with the Bauhaus, and Gropius, Moholy-Nagy, Bayer and van der Rohe all ended up in the United States. Two significant American appointments of Europeans not from the Bauhaus were that of Mehemed Fehmy Agha (1896–1978) to art director for *Vogue* (from 1929 until 1942), and Alexey Brodovitch (1898–1971) to art director for *Harper's Bazaar* (from 1934 until 1958). Although the Great Depression provided the economic backdrop to their first years on these glamour titles, their early work dramatically enlivened and accentuated the fashionable qualities of the magazines, and from this vantage point propagated new ideas in the

**Fette Fraktur** *28pt*

a b c d e f g h i j k l m
o p q r f t u v w x y z
𝕬 𝕭 𝕮 𝕯 𝕰 𝕱 𝕲 𝕳
𝕵 𝕵 𝕶 𝕷 𝕸 𝕺 𝕻 𝕼
𝕽 𝕾 𝕿 𝖀 𝖁 𝖂 𝖃 𝖄 𝟛

DEUTSCHLAND
AUSSTELLUNG 18. JULI bis 16. AUGUST 1936
*Berlin am Funkturm*
herbert bayer

Left: cover of *Deutschland Ausstellung* prospectus designed by Herbert Bayer, 1936. The Nazi-forced closure of the Bauhaus in 1933 led to the diaspora of Modern designers from Germany, spreading the new ideas. Before Bayer left for the United States in the late 1930s (in 1938 he helped organize the famous Museum of Modern Art Bauhaus exhibition in New York) he can be seen to have compromised his work with this promotion for a Nazi-organized German culture show. It uses his condensed modern (sub-Bodoni) face Bayer-type. Above: Fette Fraktur, a popular nineteenth-century black-letter and the type of face seen as essentially Germanic in the 1930s. In 1941 it was cast out by the Führer as betraying Jewish origins and also being unsuitable for imposing a global message. **p.61**

Left: the second issue of a short-lived Barcelona periodical espousing the Modern movement in architecture, and also flying the flag for a new typography. It explored an unusual square format and held firm to the grid, with Futura as the sole typeface. Below: promotion for the highly stylized face Independent from the Amsterdam Type Foundry, designed by G. Collette and J. Dufour, 1930 – a playful extreme of Deco hinting at the abstraction of character forms.

relationship of type and image. Each had worked in Paris and brought with them an awareness of Bauhaus thinking, along with the experience of the lively French commercial poster scene. Neither designed type or kept to strict rules on which types were acceptable, but both helped forge the new idea of the art director as one who directed layout, photography and illustration, rather than crafting every element. Both challenged magazine design conventions by using large photographs and white space, and sought to represent content through typographic expression.

At the Italian office equipment manufacturer Olivetti the strong design culture extended to graphics. The corporate typography was allied with ideas of industrial design and exhibition display in the work of Giovanni Pintori, Xanti

Schawinsky and Nivola, among those graphic designers who worked for Olivetti under its Development and Publicity Office, established in 1931. The relationship between the potential of type and the nature of the typewriter-written word and how those words are produced (at some point, from the imagination) is demonstrated in a 1934 folder designed by Schawinsky (a former Bauhaus student) and targeted at selling typewriters to doctors. It layers text over headline, sets type flush against a curve, dramatically contrasting typographic and photographic elements, and uses lines of type as pointers for the reader. In another Olivetti project, Schawinsky's fundamental questioning of typographic principles is flourished by the distinction of having no words other than the logotype in an image – a woman rests her hands on the petite form of a typewriter, the product's own

RIVISTA DI ESTETICA E DI TECNICA GRAFICA

ANNO 5 N. 1 . GENNAIO 1937-XV . SPEDIZIONE IN ABBON. POSTALE

DRADI-ROSSI
FOTOCOPPOLA
· BUENOS AIRES

Left: cover for *Campo Grafico* from 1937 by Attilio Rossi. This Modernist Italian designer helped found the pioneering Modern architecture journal and spread Modernist graphics to Buenos Aires when he moved there in 1935 in despair at Italian politics.

branding (the Olivetti name being boldly displayed in two places) sufficing to make the advertising statement, the image bound together by the use of the same colour for the machine and the woman's lipstick. Schawinsky was one of a number of prominent designers who worked with Antonio Boggeri (1900–90). Studio Boggeri opened in 1933 and became a focal point for new graphic design in Italy, drawing on contact with the Bauhaus set.

The foundries responded to the demand for creating "the Bauhaus look" by creating numerous sans serif and block serif faces, usually drawing on Futura, but not exclusively. Erbar was a popular geometric sans serif released during the 1920s, and Rudolf Koch's distinctive Kabel face also had followers. Key designers who added their contribution to the foundry catalogues at this time included Herbert Bayer (Bayer Type); Lucian Bernhard (Bernhard Gothic); William A. Dwiggins (Metro); Frederic Goudy (Goudy Sans); and R. Hunter Middleton (Stellar). The block serif revival followed on as, in effect, serifs were added to the Futura model to produce a new form of the traditional "Egyptian" face: Memphis, City, Beton, Cairo, Karnak, Rockwell (a revival), Pharaon and Scarab are some of those from the largest suppliers (these suppliers had the best distribution and this in turn influenced tastes). Cutting these faces was part of the response of type foundries to meet the burgeoning needs of advertising typographers as clients became more sophisticated and the demand for graphic communications increased.

Bayer-type *38pt*

a b c d e f
g h i j k l m
n o p q r s t
u v w x y z

City *21pt*

ABCDEFGHIJKLMNOPQRSTUVWXYZ
abcdefghijklmnopqrstuvwxyz

Opposite: Peignot, a highly original twist on the search for the universal alphabet, was designed by A.M. Cassandre for Deberny & Peignot, Paris, 1937. Originally distributed in three different weights, this sans serif dispensed with lower-case letters for all but "b", "d" and "f", and created a new lower case with ascenders and descenders added to capitals. Cassandre believed he had drawn a purer form of the alphabet which bore the "essential character" of roman letters. He intended Peignot for text and was disappointed at its low adoption. Left: Bayer-type, 1931, by Herbert Bayer, an experimental universal type design digitized by The Foundry, 1990s. The mono-alphabet Modern appears to have influenced the more conventional Bayer-type issued by Berthold in 1935 (used on the Bayer-designed prospectus shown on page 61). Below left: City, a 1930 design by George Trump, was a stylized take on the Modernist love of geometry. Essentially it was a fresh twist on the old slab serif. Memphis and Rockwell were other popular 1930s revivals of this type form.

A<sub>A</sub> B<sub>b</sub> C<sub>c</sub> D<sub>d</sub> E<sub>E</sub> F<sub>f</sub> G<sub>g</sub>

H<sub>H</sub> I<sub>i</sub> J<sub>j</sub> K<sub>k</sub> L<sub>l</sub> M<sub>m</sub> N<sub>N</sub>

O<sub>O</sub> P<sub>p</sub> Q<sub>Q</sub> R<sub>R</sub> S<sub>S</sub> T<sub>T</sub> U<sub>U</sub>

V<sub>V</sub> W<sub>W</sub> X<sub>X</sub> Y<sub>Y</sub> Z<sub>Z</sub>

1 2 3 4 5 6 7 8 9 0

1 2 3 4 5 6 7 8 9 0

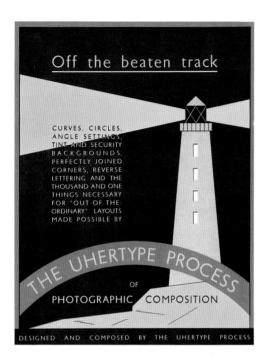

One of the most distinctive sans faces was Cassandre's Peignot for the foundry Deberny & Peignot. This questioned the existence of different forms for upper and lower case, seeking to do away with most of the different, supposedly corrupt, lower-case forms. However, as an acknowledgement of reader expectations, the face maintains the concept of ascenders and descenders and also has contrasted thick and thin strokes as a nod to ideas about legibility. Cassandre was insistent that this was not a decorative face, but a more pure form of the alphabet than tradition had led to thus far. The single alphabet concept was not carried through to its ultimate implication, however, as both upper- and lower-case forms were cut.

Not all development was so fashionable or dramatic. In the

Libra *21pt*

abcdefghij
klmnopqrs
tuvwxyz

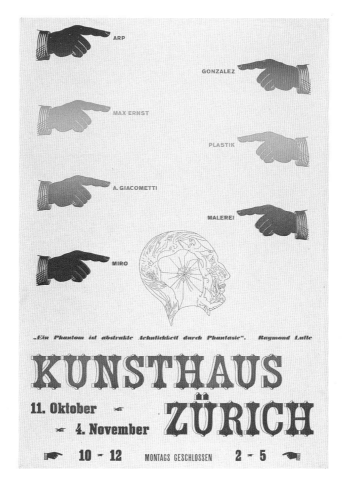

Opposite top: advertising for Uhertype photocomposition, 1939. Edmund Uher was one of the early experimenters with phototypesetting, trying manual and keyboard processes. He commissioned Jan Tschichold, among others, to design new faces for his technology in 1935, but these do not survive. Opposite centre and below: Libra, an intriguing sport from 1938 designed by S.H. de Roos for the Amsterdam Type Foundry. It draws on uncial script – the rounded letterform of early Latin manuscripts. This occasional inspiration to type designers has yet to win any popular revival. Above left: front and back cover of S. I. Kirsanov's *The Word Belongs To Kirsanov*, designed by Solomon Telingater, 1930, in Moscow. The Constructivist meets Dadaist as Telingater explores the diagonal, montage, and deliberately crude juxtapositions of different fonts, weights and sizes. Left: everyday Dada from Max Ernst in 1934 with a poster for an exhibition in Zurich. The exotic, decorative, shadowed headline type and silk-screened colours over the standard repeated printer's hands insert elaborate jokes about the vernacular within a simple composition.

design of type for text there was a search for higher standards in traditional faces, as well as faces that combined the best of the old with the ideas of the new. Stanley Morison was brought in as typographic consultant to *The Times* newspaper in London after complaining about the newspaper's setting – this despite *The Times* having a high standard among newspapers. Morison saw a text face that was inadequate for the tasks placed upon it, and a sloppy sense of typographic discipline. His advice led to a decision to go for a different but extant revival face; tests were carried out with some of Monotype's recent revivals and new faces: Plantin, Baskerville and Perpetua (Gill's latest). The drawbacks of these when used on newsprint helped Morison argue the case for a new face. It was decided that this should be based on Plantin, the main merit being that Plantin

was more condensed and took up less space than Baskerville and Perpetua.

The resulting Times New Roman is a loose revival, with reference to the sixteenth-century face of the Amsterdam printer Christophe Plantin and with key qualities of twentieth-century typeface design. Morison aimed to improve newspaper type to a quality comparable to that in average book production; in that way he would bring the finer craft standards into the realm of mass production. That few lay people would spot his changes was for him a mark of achievement, not criticism: *The Times* is said to have received only one letter of complaint after the new face was introduced in the issue of 3 October 1932. In his "First Principles of Typography" essay Morison asserted: "for a new

Caledonia *48pt*

# A B C D E F G H I
# J K L M N O P Q
# R S T U V W X Y Z
# a b c d e f g h i j k l m n
# o p q r s t u v w x y z

Above: Caledonia, 1939/41, by William Addison Dwiggins for Linotype. This re-drawing of nineteenth-century Scotch roman provided a robust, readable face that quickly gained wide use in book production, rivalled only by Times New Roman, opposite, which thanks to the extent of the British Empire became perhaps the most widely read typeface mid-century. It first appeared in 1932 in *The Times*, London, designed by Stanley Morison and Victor Lardent from the inspiration of sixteenth-century Plantin. Morison, like Dwiggins, sought to create a readable, "transparent" type.

A B C D E F G H I
J K L M N O P Q
R S T U V W X Y Z
a b c d e f g h i j k l m n
o p q r s t u v w x y z

fount to be successful, it has to be so good that only very few recognise its novelty".

In fact the font was not so successful with other newspapers as they used poorer paper than *The Times* and required type with less contrast of stroke and fineness of serif. However, it was widely adopted for books – indeed the renowned American type historian and small-press printer D. B. Updike used it for the final book from his Merrymount Press, *Some Aspects of Printing, Old and New*, in 1941. This was quite an honour for a face that Morison himself would later sum up as being "by the vice of Mammon and the misery of the machine...bigoted and narrow, mean and puritan".

Awareness of unsatisfactory standards in type in the 1920s

had led newspaper proprietors in the US to call for the likes of Linotype and Intertype to improve what was workable on their high-speed letterpress machines. Ionic, cut in 1925, was a key development, being a throwback face that drew on the Victorian Clarendons for a rugged look distinguished by an almost even stroke line and a high x-height. It was swiftly adopted by newspapers internationally. In 1931 Linotype's Excelsior came out as a design developed to overcome the ink-trap effect on counters of tighter characters. Then came Paragon and Opticon, the latter opening out its characters even more to work with heavily inked newspapers. This series was part of Linotype's Legibility Group of new faces tackling the need for a type culture specifically suited to the needs of newspapers and other large-run, low-cost text printing. The culmination of this period of development was the issue of Corona in 1941, a face that became immensely popular with American newspapers.

In the background there was the emergence of the early phototypesetting systems. Edmund Uher took out international patents for a system with both a keyboard and manually set method of instructing the exposure of type design (carried on a glass cylinder) on to photosensitive paper. Tschichold designed the promotional material and around ten faces for Uher in 1933, but none of the drawings appear to have survived after a later change of policy at the company. In 1935 a specimen book of Uhertype hand-settings was released, designed by Imre Reiner to show how flexible the process would be for innovative typography.

Spreads from *Mise en Page*, 1931, a guide to new layout ideas for the printer and the designer. Written, designed and produced by Parisian printer Albert Tolmer, it sought to blend the Bauhaus and commercial printing.

Uher's was not the only phototypesetting development. In New York, Photo-Lettering Inc. offered a service of photocomposed display lettering using the Rutherford Photo-Letter Composing Machine, launched in 1933. This machine had similarities with the Uher invention in that it used a glass slide to carry the character images, which was moved in front of the light source to expose characters, the images passing through a focusing lens on to photosensitive paper. The method and control was crude, there was still plenty of development to be done, but the basis for a new understanding of type was being born, through the embrace of photography.

This was the decade when men and women in the Western world began to see that world more through the camera, as represented in the cinema, and hear about it through their ears (radio) rather than relying on print and word of mouth. Indeed, the unsung designers of Hollywood movie titles were really getting to grips with expressive lettering as much as the celebrated heroes of modern design mentioned above. Print was still growing, but was no longer so dominant: for every daily newspaper bought in Britain (the country with the highest readership of newspapers) in the 1930s, two cinema tickets were sold.

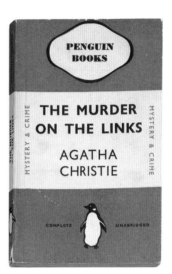

Above: early Penguin book covers from 1935 onwards. This London publisher took the paperback format upmarket and sought a new graphic language in the process. Gill Sans was used for the covers and Times New Roman for text, these new faces helping brand the offer. The publisher Allen Lane and designer Edward Young drew on the pioneering Tauchnitz editions, right, and the crisp typography and colour-coding of the Hamburg-based Albatross editions, far right, whose designer was the German/Italian fine printer and type designer Hans "Giovanni" Mardersteig.

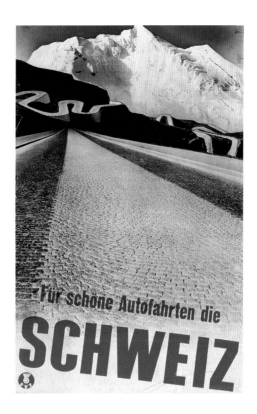

MOTOR

Nr. 7147  34 Punkte
Min. 10 kg      14 A

KUPFERBERG GOLD

Nr. 7148  40 Punkte
Min. 12 kg      10 A

VOLKSBILDUNG

Nr. 7149  48 Punkte
Min. 16       10 A

OPERNHAUS

Nr. 7150  60 Punkte
Min. 20 kg      10 A

HAMBURG

Nr. 7151  72 Punkte
Min. 26 kg       8 A

STADION

Schriftgießerei Ludwig & Mayer Frankfurt am Main

Above: two forms of a poster designed by Herbert Matter, 1935, for the Swiss tourist office. A single colour change of the red plate enables this poster to work in different languages, while the type remains integrated in the composition. The considerations of international business life are not to be under-rated as a spur to the development of form – the later success of the International Style is partly because it helped deliver efficient graphic design. Left: Motor by K. Sommer for Ludwig & Mayer, 1930 (called Dynamo in its unshaded version), is a "techno" font. It celebrates the car; now it is the computer.

L.N.E.R. Sans diagrammes

9.3.33

a b c d e f g h i j k l m n
o p q r s t u v w x y z
A B C D E F G H I
J K L M N O P Q
R S T U V W X Y Z

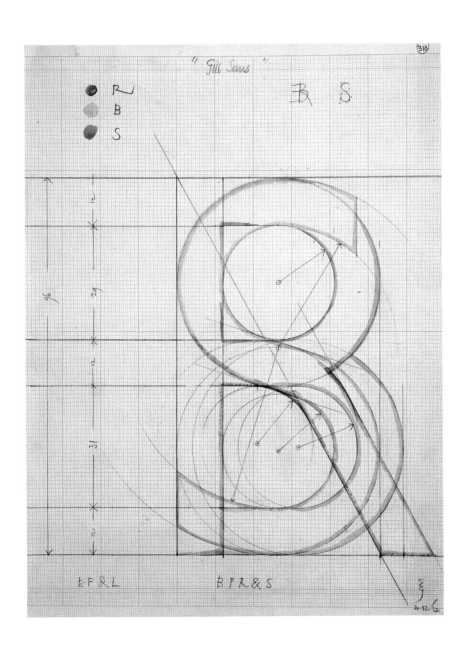

Left and opposite: drawings made by Eric Gill for the first version of his famous eponymous sans serif type, produced for the London & North Eastern Railway. One shows the "g" and was drawn in 1933; while the combined "B", "P", "R" and "S" dates from 1932. The LNER adopted Gill Sans for all signage, advertising and timetables.

40s

The Second World War delayed the advance of many ideas vaunted in the years before 1939. As resources and markets for new typefaces disappeared in the all-consuming war efforts, so too did the climate for experimentation: the early efforts at photosetting would have to wait twenty years for fulfilment, while aesthetic discussion also settled into entrenched positions for want of pioneers in education or the fuel of consumer demand for the new.

War produced its own distinct contribution to the demand for graphic design in the form of government information, particularly the propaganda poster. This was the last hurrah for the poster medium, which was increasingly undermined by the growth in magazine and newspapers and cinema, and soon to be knocked into a minority medium by the arrival of television as the means of mass communication.

The movement towards integrated image and type had taken root in much commercial work in the 1930s, but information posters were a different challenge: with scant resources, designers were often required to present complex messages that would be quickly understood. Some of the most noted posters of the period were produced by leading European designers of the prewar era – many of whom were working in exile in the US or Britain. In the US young American Modernists joined European exiles: the Office of War Information commissioned prominent designers such as the Austrian Joseph Binder, the Italian Leo Lionni and the Frenchman Jean Carlu to create posters. Exiles like Bayer and Matter, among others, produced designs for the Container Corporation of America's innovative series of promotions, in which the commercial purpose was largely subsumed within messages in support of the war effort.

The immigrant designers arrived with a vision that had an immediate impact on the American scene. A new typography acceded to power in the world's most powerful economy. The radical was becoming the mainstream. But these designers did not simply impose their beliefs; they were also changed by the experience of being accommodated within the framework of largely unfettered capitalism. This evolution would take the idealism of the 1920s into a creed of Modernist communication for the world. The brutal simplicity of high Bauhaus work developed into a more subtle, studied display of Modernist key principles. Sans type, the stripping-out of ornament and concentration on a core message gave fresh impetus to the punching out of war propaganda or commercial messages.

New York was the centre of graphic design activity and was the proving ground for the interplay of the new ideas and the vernacular. The results are apparent in the work of the "New York School" of American designers – Lester Beall (1903–69), Paul Rand (1914–97) and Bradbury Thompson (1911–95) being the most renowned. Rand's working life stretched over sixty years, from art directing *Apparel Arts*, *Direction* and then *Esquire* magazines in the late 1930s to doing corporate consultancy work for the likes of IBM and writing in the 1980s, to producing some final fiery polemics right up to the time of his death. In his work as an advertising art director at the

Weintraub agency in the 1940s he pushed the standard of advertising layouts. His partnership with Bill Bernbach (1911–72, the founder of the advertising agency Doyle Dane Bernbach) helped lay the basis of the current concept of the art director and copywriter team: where the copywriter was once king in advertising, it increasingly became apparent that a full integration of the copywriter and art director's ideas enabled a more expressive approach to be taken towards type and image, allowing them to contain the idea, not simply carry it.

In 1946 Rand published *Thoughts On Design*. This book was an influential statement of his principles and also a sign that American graphics was maturing – it no longer needed to take all its direction from the European imports. Rand's career is marked by a bringing together of ideas from fine art while advancing the argument for an almost scientific approach to the issue of legibility with type. In *Thoughts On Design* he mixed commonsense practical notes with a mystical demand for typographic and visual communications to display "the integration of the beautiful and the useful".

The high point in Bradbury Thompson's contribution to typographic thought came through his editing of the promotional publication *Westvaco Inspirations*, between 1939 and 1961. His adventurous experiments with layouts explored the processes of print and punned on the potential of type and image. But they were more than just fun: they sought out a deep appropriateness of form for the subject. Thompson also designed *Mademoiselle* magazine from 1945 to 1959, was art director of *Art News* for twenty-seven years, and later in his career became a prolific designer of fine books. But his most provocative contribution was his development of the single alphabet idea promoted by Bayer and others with the 1946 publication of his "mono alphabet". Like Bayer, Thompson proposed that only the lower-case alphabet should be used. Experimenting with Futura, his proposal included beginning sentences with a full stop and using bold instead of capitals. In 1950 he presented a further refinement on the simplified alphabet idea called Alphabet 26. Instead of the forty-five different characters that exist in the upper- and lower-case alphabets, Thompson took the twenty-six that he saw as the most distinctive symbols for each letter. He used Baskerville for the exercise to show that the project was not about radical innovation but about concentration on what is at the heart of familiar type forms.

Rationed paper, conscripted troops and the removal of other resources for print and design work restricted the designers remaining in Europe. But as in the US, there was some poster art of note: in Britain, Modernist design was encouraged when the Ministry of Information asked the young designers Tom Eckersley, Abram Games and F.H.K. Henrion to produce posters. Their work displays an illustrative style that draws on art movements from Cubism to Surrealism, but there is a fresh voice in the type: as with the American designers of the same period, there is a deliberate, playful reference to a vernacular in the lettering. Stencil cuts and Victorian-style playbill lettering found new uses, as did older sans faces and a few others.

# A B C D E F G
# H I J K L M N
# O P Q R S T U
# V W X Y Z

Above: R. Hunter Middleton's Stencil, designed in the late 1930s, was an ironic nod to a vernacular that was to become only too relevant in the next six years. Stencilled characters are emblematic of the1940s – the characters detailing military equipment, a mix of the industrial (the stencil) and the hand-crafted nature of its operation. World War made typeface production a luxury in work and in materials. Right: cover of a publication from 1942 recording the Autocar Company's production of vehicles for the war effort – an authentic stencil being used by designer Paul Rand for the effect here. Inside spreads are in a typewriter face, without margins. Brutal crops and stark contrasts in shape are given the ultimate functional flourish with a spiral binding, implying the book was more a useful manual than a self-congratulatory brochure.

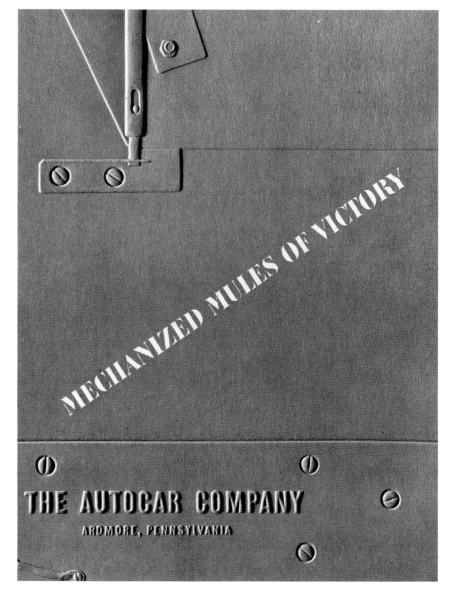

MECHANIZED MULES OF VICTORY

THE AUTOCAR COMPANY
ARDMORE, PENNSYLVANIA

There was little incorporation of the new with the old for Jan Tschichold, though. His development was an abrupt move from one to the other. During the war years his work included a series of book covers for the publisher Birkhäuser as well as research into type and calligraphic areas, the results of which appeared in his own books and articles. The Birkhäuser books are the blueprint for the work Tschichold would do when he was invited in 1946 to develop the design of the fast-growing paperback publisher, Penguin.

His impact can be seen easily by contrasting the previous Penguins with the new: new type, new spacing, even a new penguin. But the neatly centred, generously spaced, almost understated covers are unassuming from the perspective of the designer's ego – the effect is the assertion of many

classic values of book design. Besides the link with the Birkhäuser work, there is a debt to the work of Giovanni Mardersteig (1892–1977) on the 1930s Albatross books. As with the typographer and fine printer Mardersteig, Tschichold believed the key to the efficient typography of mass-production books was to devise an approach to communication, design and implementation that was rigorously applied. The Penguin Composition Rules were the result of Tschichold's concern to ensure that the various printers and typesetters who took on Penguin work would understand his requirements and work to them. Grids were produced for the different series, an innovation for the publisher. No hard and fast rules were set for typefaces – each book was tackled on its own merits, albeit jacket design elements fitted in with the identities for the various series. But every cover, title page

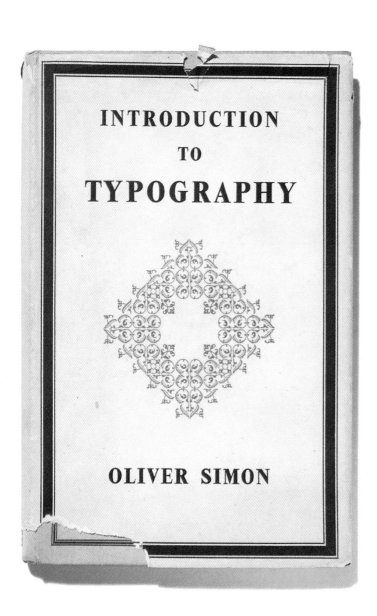

Left: Oliver Simon's *Introduction to Typography*, published 1946, was a slim bible of 138 A5 pages for the jobbing British printer. It set out the rules of quality typographic practice at the mid-century point. Below is a sample spread encouraging the proper use of printers' "flowers" – wholly at odds with Modernist thought.

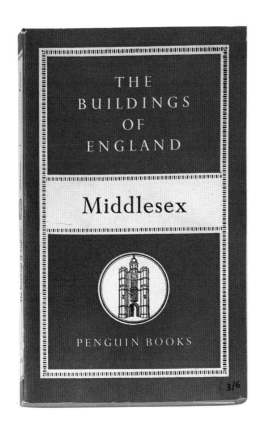

Above: Etruria Vetulonia, one of the first of the many type designs by Aldo Novarese (1920-97) for Nebiolo in Turin. Etruria was the name for the land occupied by the Etruscans, the most ancient Italian culture and a touchstone for Mussolini's rabid nationalism.

Right: Jan Tschichold's work for Penguin from 1946 demonstrated his apostasy from 1920s new typography and embrace of the fine detail of classicism. He built this into the cornerstone of a corporate identity, closely controlling the image of the various sub-brands (as here with The Buildings Of England series, and Penguin Classics) and imparting a sense of the cohesive values.

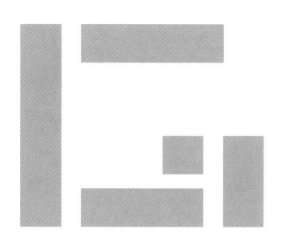

Van der Leck *24pt*

A B C D E
F G H I J K
L M N O P
Q R S T U
V W X Y Z

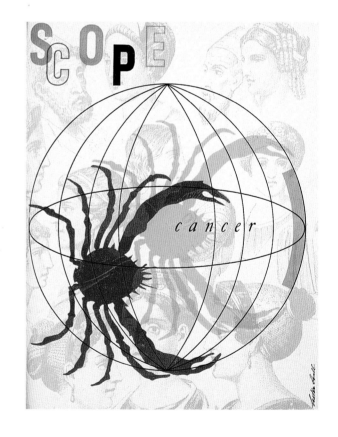

and run of body text was deemed to be part of an individual work that had to have its own coherence. Legibility, clarity and elegance were watch words. Tschichold worked on more than five hundred books before returning to Switzerland in 1949, and his rules continued to be applied after he left by his successor Hans Schmoller.

Tschichold's rejection of his earlier principles and embracing of traditional forms brought him into open conflict with the Swiss designer Max Bill. In 1946, following the report of a lecture Tschichold had given, Bill wrote an open letter attacking the "threadbare" and "reactionary" quality of Tschichold's arguments. This prompted the victim to hit back with a long reply outlining his position on Modernism versus classicism and implying that the threadbare and reactionary was appar-

ent in his critic's arguments.[1] Tschichold positions traditional typefaces and layouts as representative of a rich, organic process understood and appreciated by many and in contrast to the arcane and absolute new rules of the Modernist typography. The celebration of mechanization is attacked as a dehumanizing and essentially pointless concern. Tschichold criticizes the obsession with sans faces, saying it is fine for some display work, but is unsuitable for text. He praises the removal of superfluous elements (such as numerous faces and sizes) advocated by the new typography and recognizes its awareness of compositional quality. But, with a sense of irony, Tschichold points out that he himself set down many of the new typography rules obeyed by the likes of Bill, and asserts that he had kept to the key rules in his apparently "reactionary" move.

Bill *24pt*

abcdefghijklmnop
qrstuvwxyz

B. Tertian Malaria (plasmodium vivax)

C. Falciparum Malaria (plasmodium falciparum)

A. Malaria in the Mosquito

D. Quartan Malaria (plasmodium Malariae)

For all that there was a hiatus in new type, and a backlash against the Modernist innovations of the pre-war years, experimental lettering in the 1940s survived in pockets. Opposite left: De Stijl influenced lettering by the painter Bart van der Leck for a 1941 edition of a Hans Andersen story. Above: Max Bill's lettering for a 1949 exhibition stand, with geometry meeting calligraphy. Both these have been made into digital type Architypes in the 1990s by The Foundry in London. Opposite and left: cover (March 1948) and a spread (June 1944) from the magazine *Scope* designed by Lester Beall for the Upjohn Corporation in the United States. Beall's use of a minimal palette of typeface, in size and form, was enlivened by a masterly use of tints and of half-tones, showing the emerging opportunity for and awareness of the extra power of colour in editorial. The spread here shows the life-cycle of the malaria parasite.

Bringing together the two strands of typographic development, Tschichold acknowledged a debt to Stanley Morison and his colleagues at Monotype for the rebirth and development of classic types which had "brought with it a typographic revival the world over that is as important as the cleaning-up process of the new typography was for Germany". In 1946 the principles of the "rebirth" were crystallized in a slim volume written by the man who was instrumental in advising the choice of Tschichold for the Penguin job, Oliver Simon. In the 1920s he had edited the first four issues of *The Fleuron*, preceding those edited by Morison, and in the 1930s he had run another typographic magazine, *Signature*, as well as carrying out his work as director and typographer of the fine book printer The Curwen Press. Now, in his *Introduction To Typography*, Simon set down the principles of good practice in book typography of the kind Tschichold and Morison admired and good printers knew by heart. It was written for the young printers, publishers and other interested parties who would be involved in the rapid growth of postwar printing. It went into several editions, and was a further propagator of the orthodox standing firm against the Modernists. It did not even mention the New Typography or those designers associated with it. World conflict had ended, but design was still at war.

**Trade Gothic** *24pt*

# A B C D E F G H I J K L M N O P Q R S T U V W X Y Z
# a b c d e f g h i j k l m n o p q r s t u v w x y z

Opposite: in this poster for motor racing at Monza in Italy the foreshortened projection of the words helps create both the sense of depth and speed. Meanwhile the red, green and white suggest the colours of the Italian flag; but it is the red, blue and green speeding arrows that suggest the cars; while the green and blue are the type (suggestive of sky and countryside?). The enigmatic yet highly reduced mix of figurative and abstract makes this poster by Max Huber a masterpiece of mid-century graphics, realizing the new ways of seeing within a real commercial setting. Left: Trade Gothic, first released in 1948 by Linotype and added to in succeeding years to produce an extensive family of variations. Designed by Jackson Burke, this is a utilitarian face (condensed even in its standard form) that mixed Modernist tweaks into a basic nineteenth-century sans.

"As there are many splendid types of earlier centuries that we still gladly use in printing, it may perhaps be asked why new types are designed. Our time, however, sets the designer other tasks than did the past. A new type must, along with beauty and legibility, be adapted to the technical requirements of today, when high-speed presses and rotary presses have replaced the hand press, and machine-made paper supplanted the handmade sheet. Just as musicians and artists seek to create some new expression of our time and link it to a rich past, so too must the work of type designers and type founders remain bound to the great tradition of the alphabet."

In his 1954 book of typographic quotes and exercises, *Manuale Typographicum*, Hermann Zapf (1918–) noted the inevitable requirements for change wrought by new audiences, new media and new technology. The 1950s were the last years of hot metal's unchallenged leadership in typographic communication. By the end of the decade photosetting had gone beyond the experimental and was delivering radical change in the process of generating type.

Growing audiences for, briefly, cinema, and then the explosion of television as the mass medium of choice, threw up new challenges for the application of type and lettering that broke free of the restrictions and labours of metal setting. Movie titles of the 1950s began to integrate type and images in ways dreamt of by Moholy-Nagy in the 1920s. The work of the designer and director Saul Bass (1920–96) on films such as *The Man With The Golden Arm*, *Walk On The Wild Side*, *Psycho* and *Vertigo* fully integrated lettering and image into time-based experiences capable of setting the mood and suggesting a story. But while the creative vision was in tune with the times, the process of creating type was still stuck with materials and processes that were in keeping with nineteenth-century knowledge. Lettering for titles and other screen imagery was more easily drawn by hand than done by hot metal or handsetting, which created a proof that had to be transferred to film.

While there were many individual contributions made by designers, such as the noted typefaces of Hermann Zapf and Roger Excoffon (1910–83) (see illustration), who both explored and mixed tradition, calligraphy and modern demand in their work, this period stands out for the emergence of the school that came to dominate typographic layout worldwide – the Swiss/International Style. The designers in this group had a massive impact, projecting theories that still underpin much that is taught and practised despite years of reaction against the approach. The International Style is based on the creation of a grid for all designs, and the concentration on sans serif faces and asymmetric layouts. Its roots can be seen to relate clearly to the work of Theo Ballmer (see page 60), but it is also a derivation and pursuit of the ideals espoused by the Bauhaus and the young Tschichold, and it has links with the De Stijl artists' reduction of form to rectangular blocks and lines. One teacher in particular would later have a major influence: from 1918 until 1956 Ernst Keller taught at the Kunstgewerbeschule in Zurich (Applied Art School). Among

his early pupils were Ballmer, and later Adrian Frutiger and Edouard Hoffman (designers of the ground-breaking 1950s faces Univers and Helvetica). Keller preached clarity and simplicity, restricted styles and close letter fit. These principles aimed for communication divorced from the baggage of tradition and the clutter of unnecessary associations.

Layouts designed by Ballmer and Max Bill in the 1930s were early intimations of this approach. By splitting the page or poster into a grid, modules were arrived at that could be used to articulate clearly proportion, balance and perspective. In 1950 Bill began teaching at the Hochschule für Gestaltung in Ulm, Germany, developing a curriculum that united his background of Bauhaus training and Swiss-style schooling with an attempt at a universal statement about typography. His search for a rigorous, mathematical logic to graphic design was similar to the teaching of Emil Ruder (1914–70) in Basel around the same time, who sought to pare down the thinking of students to an appreciation of the value of white space and formal rhythms in relation to the type. He stressed that the empty space was as crucial a part of the design as the printed areas and encouraged a limited selection of faces, weights and styles. But he also appreciated novelty and dynamic qualities in layouts. This did not permit unaccountable idiosyncrasy, though. Unlike some other Swiss theorists, Ruder was not opposed to justified setting, seeing it as sometimes preferable to ragged right as it balanced blocks of text and prevented setting from being a dense mass.

Joseph Müller-Brockmann (1914–96) was a Swiss designer whose visual ability, manifested in poster work and books, gave dramatic beauty to the reductive principles behind International Style. He went further than Ruder and Bill in laying down laws, proposing "objective design" that was freed from designers' subjective expressions and taste and instead represented a purely functional communication. He opposed the combining of different type families, or even different forms of the same family. Different sizes were also to be avoided, and the type area should be as compact as possible. Line spacing should not permit any line to be isolated and inter-word spacing was to be uniform. He preferred sans serif faces for their avoidance of "decorative" contrasting stroke weight and the "ornament" of the serif, believing they functioned as well as romans for most tasks.

These views went from being essentially Swiss-based to being discussed and followed worldwide. This was partly due to the movement of influential designers around Europe and to the United States but also to the promotion of these principles in the magazine *Neue Grafik*, launched in 1959. Edited by Müller-Brockmann, Richard Lohse, Hans Neuberg and Carlo Vivarelli, it was written in German, English and French and illustrated these design principles by using the best new Swiss typography.

The argument for sans serif faces promoted by the Swiss typographers built on the earlier influence of the Bauhaus which had led all the major foundries to turn out copies of

allegro
parfum de Cléry

Left: promotional image by Roger Excoffon (1910-83) of his brush-stroke type Choc of 1953. Released by the Fonderie Olive, this was one of a series of joyful and ingenious types by Excoffon that managed to retain the sense of the calligrapher's freehand within the constraints of metal type. These brush scripts were designed primarily for advertising and quickly gained popularity, giving the opportunity for fresh expression in an era wishing to break from the drab and imposed utilitarianism of the near past.

Optima *18pt*

ABCDEFGHIJKLMNOPQRSTUVWXYZ
abcdefghijklmnopqrstuvwxyz

Melior *18pt*

ABCDEFGHIJKLMNOPQRSTUVWXYZ
abcdefghijklmnopqrstuvwxyz

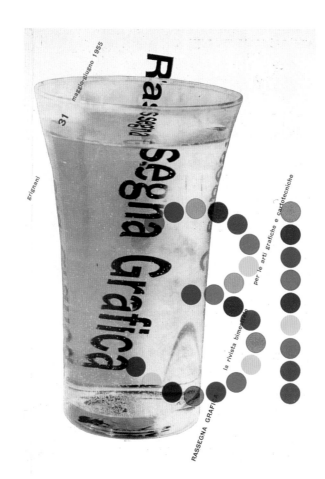

Top left: two faces by Hermann Zapf, the innovative Optima (1958) and Melior (1952). Melior was designed as a tough text face, such as on newsprint, with designs based on the rectangle. Optima explores the area between serif and sans serif, creating the stressed sans serif. Zapf's great calligraphic skills enabled him to combine modern geometric forms with the Venetian type examples he also admired, achieving a highly readable yet radical new form. Left: cover of *Rassegna Grafica*, 1955, by Franco Grignani (born 1908). The cover also demonstrates the impact that photographic manipulation was beginning to have on typography, even before photosetting arrived. Far left: the new discipline of corporate identity drew heavily on new typography in devising memorable marks that spoke of modernity. At the core of identity programmes were typographic rulebooks. Paul Rand's work for IBM, 1956, developed the existing slab serif initials, but the breakthrough point in giving character was to make the form from lines, memorably striping the whole logo block, giving it greater harmony and originality.

DANS TOUTE CONSTRUCTION

ET POUR TOUT AGENCEMENT

EQUIPEMENT NEON ASTRAL

A B C D E F G
H I J K L M N O P
BANCO
Q R S T U V W
X Y Z Æ Œ Ç É È Ê
« : ? , & . ! ; »
1 2 3 4 5 6 7 8 9 0

Above: Saul Bass (1920–96) pioneered film titles and posters as a field of evocative graphic design, producing creative ideas that worked as campaigns across film and into print. His work in the 1950s and early 1960s continues to be influential to the present day, with the above work having been taken as inspiration for at least two advertising campaigns in recent years. He combined type, calligraphy, illustration and photography – appreciating the flexibility of film and feeding that back into his print imagery.
Left: Roger Excoffon's Banco of 1951 is manifestly hand-drawn and yet suggests cut forms, strips of material laid down. Almost all his fonts were for display use, through Fonderie Olive. As a graphic designer, Excoffon saw the opportunity for more exuberant display faces in advertising (he worked for Air France among others).

Futura quickly in the late 1920s and 1930s. By the 1950s Futura and its copies had become a leading choice for advertising. Contemporary reviews of typeface usage and change of fashion in advertising noted that whereas in the UK in 1929 Cheltenham, Goudy and an unspecified sans serif grouping were first, second and third in popularity, by 1953 the figures had swapped around so that contemporary sans cuts were the first choice, followed by revived gothics, followed by Monotype's Plantin. In the US, Garamond, Caslon and Bodoni were the top three in 1929, but Bodoni, Century and Futura were leading in 1952.[1]

This demand fed the creation of Helvetica and Univers, two faces most emblematic of type design in the twentieth century. Neither could be mistaken for the product of an earlier century, but neither was so radical as to prevent quick adoption. Both were to be enormously successful. Their origin lay in the enthusiasm of designers for sans faces and the growing dissatisfaction with geometric sans serifs. It was not Futura or one of the post-Bauhaus faces that the Swiss typographers favoured above all – instead the 1896 Berthold face Akzidenz Grotesk (or Standard, in a copied version) was the constant choice of designers like Max Bill. Being a "modern gothic", Akzidenz Grotesk does not have the squared, contrasting stroke style associated with gothics such as Benton's ever-popular Franklin Gothic, and it was favoured over the geometrics for its ability to provide a more comfortable close fit of letters, with a rhythm and character the geometric faces lacked (there is a slight contrast of stroke, and tails to letters such as "a", "j", "t" and "u").

Above: the CBS "eye" logo of 1951 by Robert Golden worked across media – being a powerful device in television and in print, with a typographic pun (the C of CBS is also the pupil of the eye). Left: Alphabet 26 by Bradbury Thompson, as he presented it in Westvaco Inspirations 180, 1950. Thompson proposed merging the "best" of the upper and lower cases of Baskerville, selecting one form of a letter from each case. Capitals were set larger. Opposite: combined catalogue and exhibition poster by Marcel Duchamp, 1953. In contrast to Dadaist art, the poster is highly rational, working as advertising, but also giving a list of exhibits and four features on the event.

## DADA vs. ART

The attitude of Dada toward art is impregnated with that equivocal spirit of which Dada cultivated the ambiguity more or less wilfully, and if the irritable, imperative tone used by Dada to impose its doubt is a proof of its own dynamism, it is this very contradiction that one finds the richness of Dada's own nature.

Dada tried to destroy, not so much art, as the idea one had of art, breaking down its rigid borders, lowering its imaginary heights — subjecting them to a dependence on man, to his power — humbling art, significantly making it take its place and subordinating its value to pure movement which is also the movement of life.

I comply with your desire, dear Janis, to write you a few words on the occasion of the opening of the Dada show in your gallery, and like the actor who becomes familiarized with the role of a king, a tyrant, a criminal or a hero, I try to put myself in unison with Dada at 37 years ago. It is not easy for I have changed a great deal and am ready today to believe in angels and what was to me art at that time, seems to me today to be nature. But here is where my difficulty begins, for nature is Dada.

What you see here is Dada. You also, handsome man, beautiful woman, you are Dada, only you don't know it yourself. Tomorrow Dada will have different face from today and for that reason will be Dada. Dada is life. Dada is that which changes if would almost say the perpetual change, the eternal return. Heraclitus) Dada is life that will transform itself to morrow and behave differently from today. Dada is gay, malicious, incoherent, extremely simple, extremely complicated, practical, visible, heavy as lead, sandy, soft, square, venomous. All those paintings and sculpture, cages, chairs, windows, tables are Dada. Kees van, but are here, you are Dada as well Mary Wigman, Duchamp. Picabia, Man Ray, Ball before the pronounces of transformation "word" Dada existed. But "In the beginning was the word, that is to say in 1916 A.D. (anno Dada). Dada, in one word, is liberty. Every Dadaist was king and say anything he likes with out the risk of being hanged. Moreover the Dadaist is some times just Tzara, Huelsenbeck, Hausmann and myself were also Dadaists. It goes without saying that Marcel Janco, the Richter and Sophie Taeuber also belonged, and furthermore everyone in his turn will vanish for Dada.

### FOR THE LOVE OF DADA

This is an article for Dadaism and not against Dadaism. This is an attempt — and not the first one from my side — to take DADA seriously and reject the stupidities that have been said against it.

Was not Art (with a capital A) taking a privilege, not to say tyrannical position on the leader of values, a position which made it sever all connections with human contingencies? That is where Dada made its anti-art declaration. But inasmuch as it was expression of the individual, Dada accepted, even advocated the use of the different plastic and poetic disciplines. If Dada partly made it practice a Trojan horse to penetrate into the inner sanctum, it is, nevertheless through art realizations that Dada's criticism toward the "spiritual" institutions can be revealed as well as its device of a line of conduct and a generalized conception of vital phenomenon.

It should be noted—and this is a trait common to all its tendencies—that the artistic means of expression have, with Dada, their specific character. These means are interchangeable, they may be used in any form of art and moreover may employ incongruous elements — materials usable or looked down upon, the verbal clichés or clichés of montages, bromides, publicity slogans, refuse, etc.—these incongruous elements are transformed into an unexpected, homogeneous cohesion as soon as they take place in a newly created ensemble.

DADA was one of the great spiritual revolutions of our time. It was a real revolution of the spirit, of the mind and of the soul, and it is this revolutionary spirit that has kept it alive and justifies this exhibition.

The creation and objects of Max Ernst and Schwitters must be added chance introduced by Marcel Duchamp as a source of creation (i.e. the broken glass) and the Readymades, sort of collages of a reality superimposed upon the reality of things which no longer used the confrontation with other objects to bring out the efficacy of different aims. Dada actually used these forms of advertisement as a reality at the service of its own publicity. Schwitters constructivist period, with all its originality, is an example of this conception of Dada.

Moreover Dada, rather than merely advocating the use of its means outside of their limited purpose, spread the means and this is in my eyes the essential characteristic of Dada. The polemical meaning attached to the object was no longer descriptive or explanatory but included in its rhythmic essence, in the broken rhythm of a plot at preludes which out of the folly of analysis the dictators, bloodthirsty tyrants.

Dada is cheap and dear, like life. Dada gives itself for nothing, for Dada is priceless.

ALN ARP

(Translated by Marcel Duchamp)

1916-1923
sidney janis
15 east 57
new york
april 15
to may 9
1953

Eduard Hoffman at the Haas foundry noted the popularity of Akzidenz Grotesk and commissioned Max Miedinger to refine it and give Haas a version of it to sell: this resulted in Neue Haas Grotesk (1951–53), later renamed Helvetica when sold to Stempel (1957) and then Linotype and produced in a full family of variants. This was a face that was developed neither as an experiment nor as a punt into the marketplace, nor as a sport, nor simply as a copy of somebody else's success (although there is an element of that), but rather as a clear response to overwhelming demand. It became the most popular face for many advertising typographers, while also finding usage in text settings.

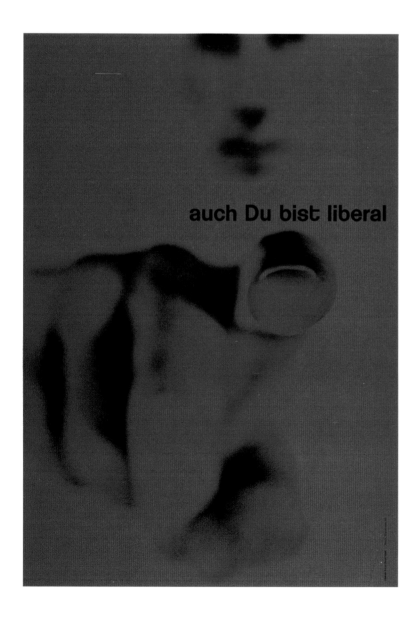

Left: "You too are liberal" poster by Karl Gerstner, 1956. Swiss style at its most reductive, with just the single bleed image taken to a hard graphic, and the brief copyline placed confidently between the focal points of the image (the finger tip and the eyes) and set in lower case except for the attention drawn to the "you" by the upper-case "D". The suggestion is clear: the subject of the piece is the viewer rather than the man pointing.

Left and above: from *Neue Grafik*.
Published 1958–66, the magazine
set out the philosophy of Swiss
Style typography, while its
ambitions to internationalism
were expressed through the use
of three languages throughout.
The journal was edited by
Zürich-based designers Josef
Müller-Brockmann, Richard
Lohse, Hans Neuberg and Carlo
Vivarelli. There is a severe
organization around the grid,
with Akzidenz Grotesk the only
face used, and just two sizes
(headline and body text). The
layout above features concert
posters by Müller-Brockmann
and the poster in the layout left
is by Eduard Müller.

**SKF**  Kugellagerbau  Vertretungen in
allen Ländern der
Welt.
Zürich  Hauptgeschäft in
Falkenstrasse 24  Göteborg.

Univers was less a market-led product and more a fulfilment of functionalist ideals – it offered an integrated family that took the basic desire for a modern, lightly stressed gothic and produced it in a comprehensive range of twenty-one variants presented in a nomenclature that attempted a revolution in type description. It was designed by Adrian Frutiger (1928–), originally as an experimental project before he was invited by the foundry Deberny & Peignot to advise on typefaces that could be transferred to photocomposition. Univers was launched in 1954 by Deberny & Peignot with a distinctive specimen sheet that presented weight and width in a logical palette, with reference numbers rather than imprecise names such as "extra bold". This idea did not catch on because printers were not interested in changing their language, however modern and logical it might be for a modern and logical face such as Univers.

Univers was distinctive in being produced in both a photosetting and a metal version. The booming demand and the new phase of type design and typographic debate of the 1950s was accompanied by radical change in the means of production. Although there had been experimentation since the turn of the century, photocomposition was not really practical until the 1950s. The process involved exposing a master negative of the characters on to photographic film in the required size. Focus, alignment, consistency of exposure and spacing had been problems before, but these were tackled until a range of competitive machines came on to the market. Different methods of storing type information were used, some using disks, some using grids. From experiments at the beginning of the decade, the systems had advanced to real commercial application by the end – in 1959, National Geographic installed the first full production model of a

Univers, designed by Adrian Frutiger for Deberny & Peignot, 1954-7. As the name suggests, it was intended to be universal, and the diagram and numbering system Frutiger devised, right, set out the principle of the 21 variations and how they related. This was a revolutionary concept for how families related, doing away with terms such as "bold", "italic", "extended" and "condensed". At the centre is Univers 55, the equivalent of standard book setting. The vertical axis shows weight, while the horizontal notes perspective. All even numbers are italic.

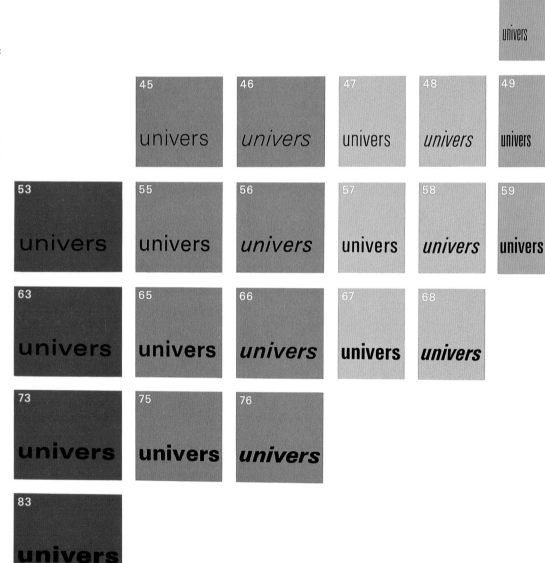

Linofilm. Photocomposition promised a cheaper, cleaner and faster way of typesetting in a form that was easily applicable to advances in film science as applied to offset lithography. But in typography the benefits would prove less certain: while the flexibility of type positioning had been improved (kerning was easier), the tendency of enlarging type to different sizes from a master, rather than holding different cuts in different sizes, would lead to the degradation of letterform quality.

Computer setting was also pioneered in this decade. It held out the prospect of saving the labours of justifying type, but it was apparent that the human eye and intelligence were not easily replaced with the achievement of consistent line setting: gaping spaces between words, and inadequate and insensitive hyphenation became associated with computer setting into the 1990s (particularly in newspapers).

Much less sophisticated, but nevertheless highly significant, Letraset instant lettering was made into a viable commercial proposition in the 1950s, the company being properly set up to exploit the process in 1959 when it offered a wet transfer method of obtaining camera-ready type. Dry transfer followed in the early 1960s. This was a vital contributor to the spirit of eclectic adventure that would in the following years shake out the staid, craftsman-like associations of graphic design, bringing typographic experimentation into the hands of anyone who could afford a sheet of rub-down letters.

**Univers 55** *24pt*

A B C D E F G H I J K L
M N O P Q R S T U V W X Y Z
a b c d e f g h i j k l m n o p q r s
t u v w x y z

ABCDEFGHIJ
KLMNO
PQRSTUVWXYZ
ÆŒÇØŞ$£
abcdefghijklmn
opqrstuvwxyz
ch ck æ œ & ß
á à â ä ã å ç é è ê ë
ğ í ì î ï ij ñ
ó ò ô ö õ ø ş ú ù û ü
. , - : ; ! ? ( [ § † ' ' * „ " « » / —
1 2 3 4 5 6 7 8 9 0

Haas'sche Schriftgießerei AG. Münchenstein

neue    haas grotesk

halbfett

wohl durchdacht, ausgewogen
diskret und temperiert,
sachlich, weich und flüssig,
mit ihren ausgefeilten,
harmonisch und logisch
aufgebauten Formen
ist die Schrift
für den täglichen Bedarf
der fortschrittlichen Druckerei

(FRITZ BÜHLER / WALTER BOSSHARD)

Helvetica roman *24pt*

# ABCDEFGHIJKLMNOPQRSTUVWXYZ
## abcdefghijklmnopqrstuvwxyz

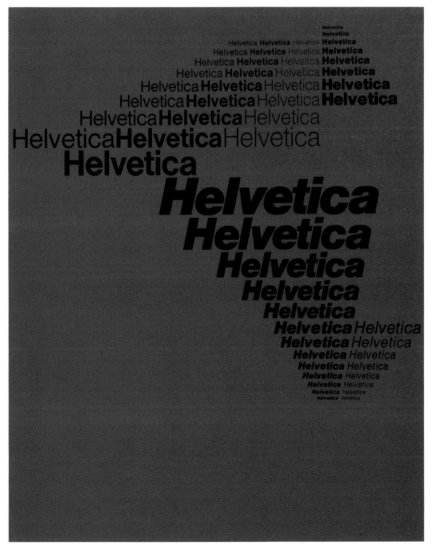

Opposite: promotional material for Neue Haas Grotesk (1958), the typeface designed to replace Akzidenz Grotesk in the favour of Swiss designers. Eduard Hoffman of the Haas foundry asked in-house designer Max Miedinger to develop the face, which has a higher x-height than AG and takes slight influence from the more geometric sans serifs that had come after the then 50-year-old AG. Designed by Miedinger and Hoffman in 1951-53, it was licensed to Stempel and to Linotype, who renamed it Helvetica (Latin for Switzerland). Left: an early 1960s promotional piece for Helvetica. In the 1960s Helvetica rose to become the most popular of all sans serifs, with its modern cut aided by a name that tied in with a belief in Swiss graphics.

Fatigue

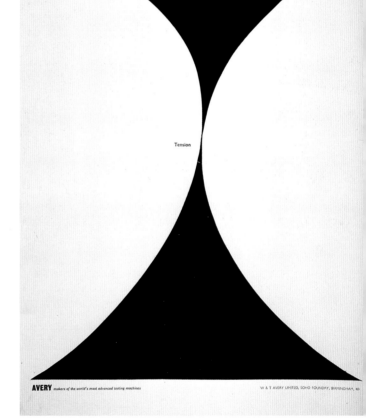

Tension

Opposite: during the 1950s advertising design began to move forward, as the growth in printed material and competitive advertising demanded more brand difference to be demarcated graphically. Gradually, more radical ads started to emerge, few more extreme than these press advertisements from the W. S. Crawford agency in London, designed by Paul Peter Piech. A remarkable absence of type or of product shots opens the way for powerful abstract forms to be used to illustrate the concepts behind the value of Avery scales. A single word – "tension" or "fatigue" – is expressed in black and white composition. Piech, an American soldier who stayed in Britain after the war, later worked on personal posters without type, shaping his own linocut letters. Right: an advertisement for the Italian printers Alfieri & Lacroix, 1960, by Franco Grignani, explores the flexibility of film to express the motion of the press by rotating and reversing the name of the advertiser.

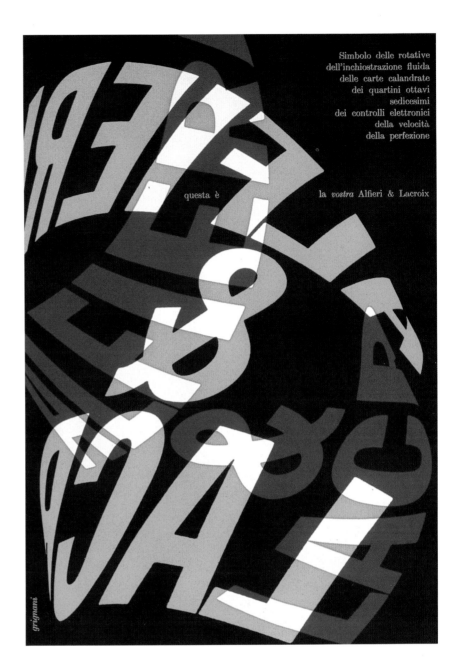

MICHAEL

FOR A TYPOGRAPHICAL CELEBRATION OF THE 1960S, M/M (PARIS, FRANCE) OFFERS YOU A TYPOGRAP
AND MATHIAS (BORN THE 04/04/1967) EXECUTED FOR 280FF (£32) IN FRONT OF THE POMPIDOU CEN

THIAS

DIGITAL REMASTERISED VERSION OF A PORTRAIT OF MICHAEL (BORN THE 02/06/1968
PARIS, FRANCE) BY AN ANONYMOUS ARTIST (ON THE 18/03/1995). THANK YOU!

The emerging force of "youth culture", the rapid growth of television and change in type technology made this a decade that would re-invent the nature of typography. Unlike the radical experiments of the 1920s, in this period the scientific, social and political shifts prompted typographic novelty.

From the late 1950s onward there was a rush to market photocomposition machines: some found success and helped the development of new companies that supported type design programmes (such as Compugraphic and Hell); some met with failure – notably American Type Founders, which emerged at the end of the nineteenth century from the implications of hot metal, but disappeared under a takeover from Lanston Monotype after an unsuccessful investment in its own photocomposition machine.

The uncertainty of business was due to more than changing production methods. The type consumers, the publishers and their designers, were taking in new influences and were pushing for effects that were difficult to achieve with metal, while also being prepared to see a loss of some traditional qualities of metal setting because of cost or other practical and non-aesthetic reasons. That photosetting led to a drop in typographic skill was often lamented, but it was a chosen consequence. Suddenly type was becoming a flexible right-reading image that could easily be photographically manipulated, instead of being a rigid, wrong-reading relief letterform. Characters could be enlarged or shrunk, kerned or spaced almost at will, overlapped and positioned in a few moments rather than through hours of setting and construction on the printer's stone.

All this was encouraging for those seeking novelty and was dispiriting for those concerned with the traditional details. Poor fit of letters and ugly letterforms began to be seen, fed by the practice of generating a whole range of point sizes out of a single matrix, which inevitably distorted the face. It was also perpetuated by the ignorance of the user: with hot metal, much skill resided with the compositor, skill that a typographic designer could rely on, even take for granted to some extent. Niceties such as ligatures disappeared, partly because the ease of kerning should have overcome some of their need, partly because character sets did not extend that far, but it was a point that fine typographers missed.

The new systems began to chip away at the knowledge base of the compositor, bringing them closer to a glorified typist. Initially cold composition worked in a similar way to a Monotype machine, in that it produced a tape that drove the setting machine (but the subsequent setting was not as easily corrected: a new piece of film bromide being required to change one letter, rather than the insertion of the single letter). During the 1960s, though, computers began to impact upon this operation, offering systems programmed to assist with the justification of setting and memories that could deliver an image on a CRT (cathode ray tube) screen as reference. But this reliance on early computer programs brought problems, too, with the programmers and their systems often being unable to offer the spacing and word-break control that a good compositor would have supplied

previously. Nevertheless, hot metal was increasingly frozen out by the costs and convenience of cold type, matched by the growing drift from letterpress printing to offset lithography, which was better suited to meet the growth in quality and demand for colour printing.

There were other signs of how increasing demand for print and business communication and new methods of satisfying it threatened the print establishment. In 1961 the IBM Selectric golfball typewriter was launched, offering an office machine with the capability of changing its characters to a different face: an early sign of the move of improved output into the hands of the office worker and a step towards today's desktop publishing systems.

Another development, launched in 1961, had more creative impact – Letraset's instant dry transfer lettering. The company had marketed wet transfer lettering from 1959, but failed to crack the American market. The dry method was cleaner and simpler to use and succeeded in the US: designers realized it empowered them to produce the artwork for headlines and other display elements, bringing down time and costs; indeed, it brought fancy display setting into the reach of many areas that would never have had access to it. Early Letraset advertising presented it as something for everyone, suggesting that typography was open to anybody. One over-enthusiastic piece of copywriting even stated that there was "no talent needed" to achieve fine results.

Letraset's library grew quickly, not just with copies of existing faces (often good cuts, taken under license from the original foundry drawings), but also under its own design programme. The first, and one of the most distinctive period faces, was Countdown. Designed by Colin Brignall, who went on to be appointed design director at the company, the face suggests 1960s science fiction and was the inspiration for many shop signs, particularly boutiques that wanted to shout their futuristic modernity. Other wacky faces were produced that may now seem ephemeral gimmicks but were notable in their quick response to the spirit of the age. Letraset had an impact on everything from magazines to posters, mass advertising to local newsletters. The company also worked to commission for companies that required their logo and other artwork in rubdown form. The lettering was much used in television, being ideal for producing titles and information graphics.

Technological change supported a questioning climate for design that was fuelled by the ending of postwar austerity in Europe and came as a reaction to the brasher consumerism of the 1950s in the US. Pop Art, the major art movement of the time, was built out of or against the dominance of abstraction, and many of the artists who came to be grouped under the label used elements of vernacular typographic and popular graphics within their work (processed into paint on canvas by Andy Warhol, Roy Lichtenstein and Robert Indiana in the US, and earlier, in montage by Eduardo Paolozzi and Richard Hamilton in Britain). The ironies, mixture of visual and verbal wit, and

ABCDEFGHIJKLMNOPQRSTUVWXZ
abcdefghijklmnopqrstuvwxyz

right now!
Jackie
McLean

STEREO
THE FINEST IN JAZZ SINCE 1939
84215 BLUE NOTE

Larry Willis/Bob Cranshaw/Clifford Jarvis

Top: Roger Excoffon's Antique Olive was an attempt to offer a more refined sans serif than that presented by Helvetica and Univers – but it was too characterful and too late to be adopted widely outside France. It has a more calligraphic line than its rivals. Left: record sleeve by Reid Miles for Blue Note records, from 1964-5. Miles used type in highly inventive ways to illustrate the sleeves he created for the jazz label from 1954-69. He explored many forms of type or lettering technology, here grossly enlarging and reworking an image originated on a typewriter.

**p.105**

CHARLES TOLLIVER HERBIE HANCOCK CECIL McBEE ROY HAYNES

JACKIE McLEAN

STEREO
84179 BLUE NOTE

"it's time!"...!!!!!!!!
!!!!!!!!!!!!!!!!!!!!!!!!!
!!!!!!!!!!!!!!!!!!!!!!!!!
!!!!!!!!!!!!!!!!!!!!!!!!!
!!!!!!!!!!!!!!!!!!!!!!!!!
!!!!!!!!!!!!!!!!!!!!!!!!!
!!!!!!!!!!!!!!!!!!!!!!!!!
!!!!!!!!!!!!!!!!!!!!!!!!!
!!!!!!!!!!!!!!!!!!!!!!!!!
!!!!!!!!!!!!!!!!!!!!!!!!!

JOE HENDERSON
Kenny Dorham Richard Davis Elvin Jones etc.

STEREO
84166 BLUE NOTE

in'n
out

Eurostile *24pt*

ABCDEFGHIJKLMNOPQRSTUVWXYZ

abcdefghijklmnopqrstuvwxyz

ABCDEF
GHIJKLM
NOPQRS
TUVXYZ
W abcdef
ghijklmno
pqrstuvx
yzw 1234
567890

EUROSTILE (NEBIOLO) DISEGNATO DA A. NOVARESE - 1962

316

Gli esempi che abbiamo raggruppati sotto il titolo: « forme quadrate », sono tipiche espressioni della tendenza del nostro secolo, e sono sorte per ambientare il carattere all'estetica architetturale contemporanea.

La forma quadrata e compatta, infatti, ci è ormai familiare: essa è presente, direi, predominante, in ogni cosa che ci circonda. Ed il carattere, oggi — come fu per il passato — si fonde e si mimetizza nelle espressioni dell'epoca attuale. Gli esempi, anche pregevoli, delle pagine d'un tempo dimostrano che ogni stile — sia esso bodoniano, veneziano, egiziano, o lineare — può modificare, cambiare forma, specialmente per quanto riguarda le curve, passando da quelle tondeggianti a quelle più angolose e quadrate, senza alterare di molto l'originaria forma.

HO
ho
ho

La forma quadrata è tipica espressione architettonica del nostro secolo, come lo fu l'arco a tutto sesto dal quale derivò il carattere lapidario romano; ed anche l'arco a sesto acuto che originò, a sua volta, il carattere gotico.

317

exploration of throw-away consumer culture found in much of this work is echoed in the puns and ironies introduced into graphic communication at the time. Advertising was at the fore in expressing this change, the "golden age" of "big idea" advertising in America being led by the work of the agency Doyle Dane Bernbach. The Volkswagen Beetle campaign, which began in the late 1950s and ran through the 1960s, not only shook up car advertising by puncturing the hype of others in a self-effacing pitch, but projected this attitude in clean, restrained typography. The use of a specially cut geometric sans (based on Futura) suggested the modern, German origins of the car and the sense of good engineering. Type was being used for its cultural associations, not its inherent graphic qualities or legibility. Similarly, in DDB's ads for Levy's rye bread, the thick, soft

but strong contours of Cooper Black suggest the wholesome product.

A new adventurous expressiveness was apparent in the work of many of the leading graphic designers of the era. Reid Miles' work as art director of record covers for the Blue Note label from the mid-1950s through the 1960s developed an increasingly strong relationship between type, layout and photography, with sympathetic play between the elements, often chopping up type or photography, often merging the two. These techniques were startlingly advanced compared with many of the other sleeves in the rack. The strength of the work reinforced the whole label's identity, and heralded the realization in the music industry that graphics could sell the music, rather than just showcase the recording artist.

## Lemon.

Opposite top: two more Reid Miles covers for Blue Note (see previous caption also). Despite not being much of a jazz fan, Miles improvised around the words of a title or an artist's name in a way not dissimilar to the method of themes being explored in a jazz composition. Opposite: Eurostile, designed by Aldo Novarese in 1962 for Nebiolo, with the explanatory display he created for it in his book *Alfa Beta*. He shows how it is in keeping with the design of the age – with modern buildings, trains and television screens – rather than the classical or gothic characters of earlier type. Left: New York advertising swung into its heyday in the 1960s, with the apotheosis of the "Big Idea", and none bigger than in the Volkswagen campaign, from which "Lemon" is one of the most famous ads. The typographic identity of this work still survives in contemporary VW ads, the special cut of Futura semi-bold suggesting some Germanic know-how. The consistency of keeping the type "cool" when advertising is usually "hot" has given VW a very distinct identity.

Herb Lubalin (1918–81), who moved across from an advertising background in the 1950s to a type design career in the 1970s, produced some of his most memorable work in the 1960s, often through the reliance on typographic puns to reinforce a strong concept. His famous proposed magazine logo "Mother & Child", in which the child is an ampersand sitting in the bowl – or womb – of the "o" in mother, is trite, but saved by the perfect matching of the visual forms. Indeed, much of the visual punning of the period can seem rather laboured, but the best work goes beyond this to explore the double meanings, the ironies possible when presenting imagery to an audience that was becoming increasingly sophisticated – and jaded – in its consumption of mass communication.

The typography used in conceptual American advertising by its numerous art directors crossed the Atlantic and found its strongest response in Britain, notably with the partnership of Alan Fletcher, Colin Forbes and Bob Gill (the origins of the design group Pentagram). Their work displayed a similar ability to reduce the statement of a piece of commercial art to a key point that was boldly presented, often through typographic wit. This reductive, conceptualizing approach was a new influence overlaid on the still advancing Swiss school and the International Style. For ordering a mass of information and sorting out a typographic hierarchy, the commandments of Müller-Brockmann and his colleagues on *Neue Grafik* promised a revelation of the underlying order within a brief, a way of containing the given material clearly and with a logic. It was a creed that increasingly sat at odds with the *laissez faire* graphics of popular culture. The rules of International Style did not provide a method for popular entertainment, which commercial communication demanded increasingly, as it was realized that to stand out amidst the growing mass of mass communication, advertising needed to appeal, not hector.

A key development of the 1960s was the flowering of the phenomenon since labelled "youth culture" – the culture created by and for teenagers and twenty-somethings, products of the postwar baby boom and a generation crucially free from the experience of war and the values of the earlier era. The spending power of this group differed markedly from antecedent youth as they benefitted from near full employment and a general rise in living standards, and

A READER'S DIGEST
PUBLICATION

Avant Garde *24pt*

ABCDEFGHIJKLMNOPQRSTUVWXYZ
abcdefghijklmnopqrstuvwxyz

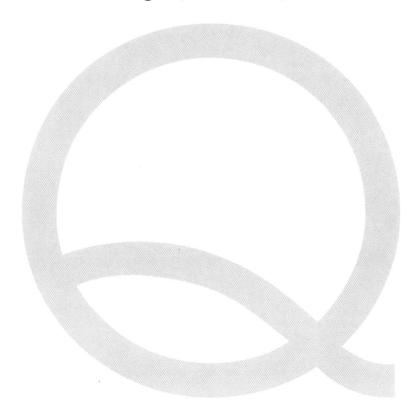

Opposite left: logo for the 1968 Olympics in Mexico, designed by Lance Wyman. International Style, psychedelia and an attempt to draw from the bold stripes in traditional Mexican patterns all converge. The mark was at the heart of a programme praised for its comprehensive approach to the huge event. Opposite right: cover of *Avant Garde* magazine, designed by Herb Lubalin. His art direction of the magazine led him to create the face Avant Garde (left), which is remarkable for its ligatures and tight fit. The incredibly close characters are typical of Lubalin's work – seen also in the masthead he created for *Families* magazine (above left). Top: advertisement for the Photo Typositor system, 1961, plays with effects and tricks popular also in early digital typography.

they displayed a growing desire to stake their own place in society. This found graphic expression most notably through music and fashion, the hot industries in free-market capitalism which now emerged as standard-bearers for the avant-garde in communication, a position they have retained.

In the mid and late 1960s, record sleeves branched out into a whole range of eclectic type designs, often borrowing ideas and imagery and redrawing letters (Letraset was invaluable). Calligraphy (of a kind) was revived with strange new psychedelic twists courtesy of airbrush artists. "Underground" magazines and other expressions of protest broke the rules wilfully: articles in the magazine *Oz*, for example, could and did appear with almost unreadably long lines, ranged right with a ragged left stepping out, and all this

This page: 1960s counter culture, particularly around rock music, developed its own graphic expression, utilizing silk-screen printing for psychedelic posters. The leading work came out of San Francisco. Clockwise from right: Procol Harum at the Fillmore by Lee Conklin; The Doors at the Avalon Ballroom by Victor Moscoso; The Yardbirds, The Doors and others, by B. McLean. The power of the incredible silk-screen colours is only hinted at by photography and four-colour process print.

reversed from a sludgy photograph. The point was not to read it in a hurry, or perhaps at all: the protest was in the way it looked. Typewriter text was popular, partly because it avoided typesetting and was thus accessible and cheap for offset lithography, but it also contained the right associations in rejecting a smart business image.

Poster art for rock concerts and festivals produced some of the most remarkable, unreadable but communicative, calligraphy, with elaborate hand-drawn or photographically stretched words suggestive of the tricks of distortion that computers and photocopiers would make much easier to explore a few years later. Victor Moscoso and Wes Wilson's psychedelic posters in the US were the most polished examples, although it was a style widely copied, with different

variations – in Britain, a revival of Art Nouveau led to an expansion of the florid lettering of that period into more psychedelic forms.

In magazine work one of the most influential practitioners was Willy Fleckhaus (1925–83). His design of *Twen* through the 1960s showed the art director in the ascendant (Fleckhaus trained as a journalist and his input in the magazine extended into the origination of ideas and treatments). He ferociously cropped photography for dramatic effect, cleared body copy from visual spreads and on to dump pages of solid text, and used blocks of type as building blocks to construct the page, suggest the grid, or challenge order. Dramatic contrasts in the scale of type often added tension to the page, with Fleckhaus elaborately

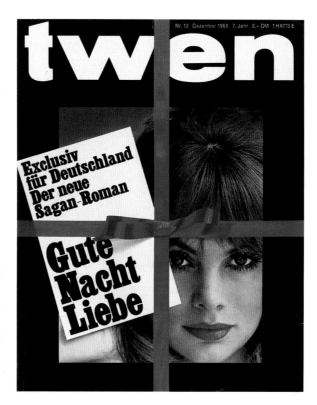

Far left: cover of promotional brochure for *Ad Lib*, designed by Freeman Craw for American Type Founders in 1961. This display face drew on nineteenth-century wood letter and the idea of the crude paper cut shapes. Craw offered alternate letters, with variations that even allowed letters to be turned upside-down without losing alignment. His was a reaction against the neutrality of modern sans serifs and a questioning of conventions, that finds an echo in the organic, "random" fonts of the 1990s. Above left: *Twen*, December 1965, art directed by Willy Fleckhaus, an art director's art director who emphasized photography and tended to consign typography to a means of text delivery.

cutting and adjusting type to fit his intentions and the space allotted. In Britain, echoes of this work could be seen in the fresh look of *Nova* magazine, which also targeted the younger set with provocative features that devoted opening spreads to strong photography, paring the text back and playing with different typefaces to convey a more emotive kick to the beginning of an article and merge more fluidly with the illustrative content.

Fleckhaus designed book covers for the publisher Suhrkamp which were exclusively typographic, the type on or out of a deliberately restricted palette of background colours. Despite the simplicity of the elements to which he confined himself, he produced highly expressive and varied covers, all reinforcing a distinct identity for the publisher.

OCR-A *18pt*

ABCDEFGHIJKLM
NOPQRZTUVWXYZ
abcdefghijklm
nopqrstuvwxyz

OCR-B *18pt*

ABCDEFGHIJKLM
NOPQRSTUVWXYZ
abcdefghijklm
nopqrstuvwxyz

CMC7 *24pt*

E13B *36pt*

But it was not all about a quest for personal or corporate individualism. The decade also saw international alignments of experts collaborating on communications technology. Committees considered research on computer-type (optical character reading). OCR–A was issued in 1966: it is an extremely coarse design, with characters produced on a 4 by 7 grid. OCR-B, issued in 1968 (with Adrian Frutiger as a consultant) works to a finer grid (18 by 25), enabling more sophisticated curves. OCR-A and its forerunner, E13B (used by banks on cheques), were a genuine machine-driven aesthetic that found a stylistic echo in the aforementioned Countdown or the more elegantly squared-off designs of Aldo Novarese's Eurostile, extended from his earlier Microgramma.

There were advances in faces that could work for screen display as well as input. Here, simplicity was used not only to create distinctions that the machine could read but to make clear forms that the human eye could swiftly assimilate. The Dutch designer Wim Crouwel (1928–) was committed to the idea that in the not too distant future the screen would be the pre-eminent source of typographic communication and was concerned that more effort should go into developing appropriate designs. His Neue Alphabet of 1967 simplified the alphabet to horizontal and vertical elements, removing diagonals and curves. All characters are the same width, and to make "m" and "w" he had to underline the "n" and "v", respectively. There was only one alphabet, not an upper and lower case.

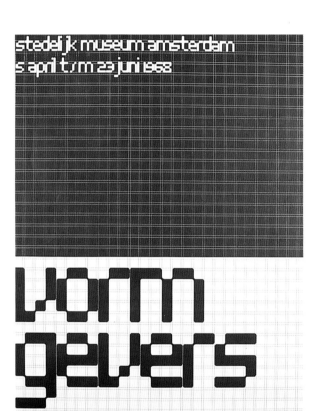

New Alphabet *40pt*

The development of computers that could read led to, first, computer-readable code, then typefaces that could be read by intermediate technologies, before gradually spawning an aesthetic. Opposite: CMC7 was a face developed for use with magnetic inks in the early 1960s (designer unknown). It was only briefly promoted, being quickly superseded. E13B was a machine-recognized set of numerals developed by the American Bankers' Association in the mid-1960s and is still seen on cheque books in the 1990s. The minimal grid idea links with that behind the poster of 1968, left (which inspired our cover) designed by Wim Crouwel (born 1928). In 1967 Crouwel designed the minimalist New Alphabet, which reduces characters to essential distinguishing elements. Opposite top: OCR-A and OCR-B came as a result of standards laid down in 1965 by the European Computer Manufacturers Association for computer-readable type. ECMA engineers developed OCR-A in 1966, while OCR-B emerged with Adrian Frutiger's assistance in 1968 – a finer face that demands greater processing power.

But with all this talk of technological change and of "Swingin' Sixties" libertarianism, what did the traditionalists think? One could always rely on Stanley Morison, responsible for reviving classic faces at Monotype, to present a sober argument for classical values. In a 1967 new edition of his 1930 essay "First Principles of Typography", he added a response to International Style and to the new wave of sans serif faces:

"Claims are made that the style appropriate for the time consists not only in the choice of sans serif type but that it be composed in asymmetrical form, without recourse to italics. Paragraphs are to be closely set without indentation, and the whole appearance of the page must depart wherever possible from age-old custom. The twentieth century would thus mark itself off by its distinctive typography as the great period of revaluation....Tradition itself is not well understood at the present day in some quarters. If it were a reflection of the stagnation or prejudice of past ages of printers, little attention need be given to it by historians and none by practitioners of the arts and crafts. But tradition is more than the embalming of forms customary in states that have been long since cast aside. The sum of experience accumulated in more than one man's lifetime, and unified by succeeding generations, is not to be safely discarded. Tradition, therefore, is another name for unanimity about fundamentals which has been brought into being by the trials, errors and corrections of many centuries. *Experientia docet.*"

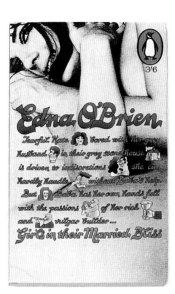

Sabon *24pt*

# ABCDEFGHIJKLMNOPQRSTUVWXYZ
# abcdefghijklmnopqrstuvwxyz

Appropriately perhaps, Morison ended on a note that, with the decline in a classical education, would be savoured by few of the new generation of typographers. For them, the reality of the typographic context was increasingly of non-print media, of communication that mixed the alphabet with sound and motion in the full fluidity of film and video and, soon, computer-based communication.

Right: Letraset's transfer lettering was quick, cheap and could even be fun – truly type for the Pop era. Faces included Milton Glaser's Baby Teeth and creative director Colin Brignall's Countdown, ready-to-rub for sci-fi covers and fashion boutiques. Opposite: commercial graphics exploded into brighter colours as print technology improved in the 1960s and Western markets became more consumer-driven. Here cutting through the noise was a Shredded Wheat pack by British design trio Fletcher Forbes Gill, a reaction that said "value" against over-packaging. Even Penguin books caught the marketing bug, allowing new art director Alan Aldridge to try more varied directions (the cover near left is his design, while Romek Marber and Alan Spain designed *Killer's Wedge*, both 1964). In 1967 he resigned when a rigorous typographic scheme was reasserted. Opposite below: Sabon, 1966, by Jan Tschichold. Just as hot metal was about to be replaced by photosetting, a group of German printers asked Tschichold to create a "unified" face that worked across both Monotype and Linotype hot metal systems and also in foundry type for handsetting. Monotype Garamond was the basis for this difficult marriage.

The 1970s have been dubbed "the decade that fashion forgot" and this label might also be extended to graphics. But with due warning: anything that seems irredeemable is usually soon to be recycled, and in music and fashion some aspects of this decade already have been. It might be a while before ITC Souvenir becomes widely used again, but don't count it out.

While rock music and clothing stretched the late 1960s visions, so in typography the promise of the preceding years turned to baroque extravagance. Experimentation with the new systems led to type being spaced so tightly that letters overlapped and words became squeezed and only semi-legible. Whatever its merits and faults, it created a distinctly contemporary form.

There was perhaps more to tight letterspacing than fashion jumping on to a new technique. Underlying some experimentation is the continuing quest for archetypal letterforms. The idea that sans serif faces produced the most functional letterforms was reinforced by a technology that increased their legibility. An argument for serifs is that they help guide the eye along the line and join letters into words, but as photo-composition provided potential for closing up sans serif faces into tight "word images", it gave new material to arguments on the relative readability of forms.

For all Modernism's love of geometric forms, such geometry bears no inherent relationship to the nature of the alphabet, which was drawn from calligraphic and (much earlier) pictogram roots. In the 1970s Adrian Frutiger demonstrated that when characters from some widely read typefaces were overlaid (Garamond, Baskerville, Bodoni, Times, Palatino, Optima and Helvetica), the skeletal forms that emerged from the superimpositions corresponded closely to faces then used in mass-market newspapers (Excelsior, Caledonia). The sans serifs Helvetica and Univers matched the basic outline exactly, but deviated, of course, in lacking serifs and having a more constant stroke thickness. For Frutiger, this illustrated that "the foundations of legibility are like a crystallization, formed by hundreds of years of use of selected, distinctive typefaces. The usable forms that have stood the test of time are perhaps permanently accepted by humankind as standards conforming to aesthetic laws." He pointed out that "where there are excessive innovations of form or designs of poor quality, the typeface encounters a certain resistance in the reader and the reading process is hindered."[1]

Note the concern about "designs of poor quality". Manufacturers had rushed to offer an impressive range of familiar faces on their phototypesetting systems, plus whatever was new and different. This led to the supply of many poorly drawn faces. There were the inevitable distortions resulting from not supplying masters in different sizes but instead requiring one size to be enlarged to all sizes. This meant that the need for a change of balance in a cut at different sizes to preserve characteristics was ignored. The decline in typographic quality was not only the result of the methods of generating type, but also of printing: the transfer of most printing from letterpress to offset lithography, as well

as the advent of inkjet and laser printing technology, unleashed type in areas where traditional typographic controls and skills were absent.

But there was a growing awareness of the graphic design *profession*. In type this was signified by the arrival of a type producer that expressed both the changing needs of the type specifier and the potential of the technology – the International Typeface Corporation. ITC was formed in 1970 by designers Herb Lubalin and Aaron Burns who joined forces with Ed Rondthaler, of Photo-Lettering Inc., to set up a company that would market new typeface designs as artwork supplied to other type and typesetting equipment manufacturers. In effect, ITC was a type design agency, building on the expertise and archive that the Lubalin and Burns partnership had already created, but also bringing in new designers and designs to license across manufacturers. Royalties would be paid on the usage of the face, and the success of the design would directly benefit its creator. This model, with adaptation, has inspired the subsequent growth of designer-led type distribution companies.

This organization responded to the prevailing trend of piracy in new typeface design. If one supplier had a design that another did not have, photo-technology made it easy to duplicate the master matrix of characters and re-name the design and then avoid paying any royalties to the originators of that face. It was not in the interests of good typeface designers or manufacturers for such a situation to continue, but neither was it desirable or practical to expect good designs to be tied to only one system.

ITC's type library began in 1971 with Lubalin's Avant Garde Gothic, drawn from his work for *Avant Garde* magazine in the 1960s. Next was a recut extended family designed by Ed Benguiat of a turn-of-the-century design, the notorious Souvenir, originally carried by American Type Founders (which had effectively disappeared in 1970 with the merger with Lanston Monotype). New faces, recut faces and extended families poured forth thereafter. ITC was a publisher, not a seller of systems – this was a radical new model for type distribution, Letraset excepted. Each new face was effectively a new title and needed to perform through different retailers (or type manufacturers) for ITC to be profitable.

In the 1973 launch edition of its own publication, *U&lc* magazine, ITC began a campaign against type piracy. An article by Rondthaler admitted that copying faces was as old as typefounding itself (and was certainly very much a part of the hot-metal era) but insisted that it was only the arrival of "phototypography" that had brought the time and costs down to the point where the pirating of type became a real threat to the origination of new work. He commented that "photography has been the technological salvation of the typesetting business, but when used unethically it can rob the type designer of his livelihood. It can do worse than that. It is now threatening to throw the creative arm of the industry into chaos." He called for designers to boycott suppliers who did not use properly licensed designs and compared the use of anything else as being akin to passing off counterfeit money. Without

A Fox is quick (0 to 50 in 10 seconds). It's surefooted (front-wheel drive). This sly, cunning sedan can take the sharpest turns nimbly (sports car type steering and suspension). It can stop practically in its tracks (power front disc brakes). And it doesn't eat much (23 miles per gallon). Best of all, for under $3,200*you can catch the Fox.

## YOUR HUNT iS OVER. THE QUiCK, SLY, CRAFTY, CUNNiNG FOX BY AUDi iS HERE.

Herb Lubalin acclaimed this early 1970s use of his Avant Garde. He praised the DDB art director Helmut Krone for setting the headline so tight that the letters join up and overlap.

strong action, warned Rondthaler, there was no reason why designers, foundries or manufacturers should consider investing in the design of new typefaces. The 1970s could either mark the demise of type design or the beginning of a renaissance, he concluded.

As it turned out, the latter was the case. There were moves in international copyright law to clamp down on such piracy, and there were followers of ITC's initiative – other type licensing enterprises and new manufacturers such as Hell and Compugraphic – investing in design. ITC's practices were not uncritically received, however; the ubiquity of its faces meant that if it marketed a bad design, then that could end up being widely adopted at the cost of a better, earlier precedent. The American graphic designer Paula

Scher later commented that "ITC had an enormous impact in this country because it was a national type business. It sold to all the small suppliers, but it destroyed the face of Garamond and it destroyed the face of Bookman."[2] ITC designs tended to have a large x-height (which aided readability in smaller sizes) and a close character fit, restrictions that eroded many distinguishing qualities of classic designs.

The high ground of detailed care in transferring and evolving type design was held by Berthold, and the torch was carried by Gerhard Lange, whose career began in 1950 and lasted into the 1990s. He oversaw the creation of a library of classic faces transferred first to photosetting, and later to digital form. Berthold's "diatronic" system of photosetting, with a

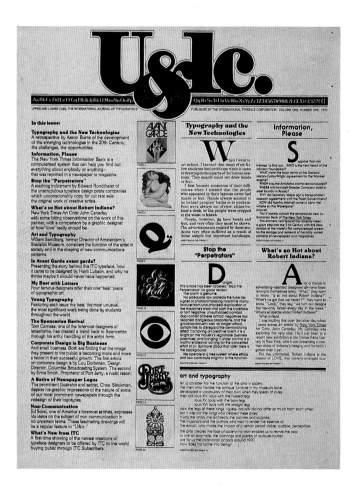

Souvenir *18pt*

# ABCDEFGHIJKLM NOPQRSTUVWXYZ abcdefghijklm nopqrstuvwxyz *y*

Serif Gothic *18pt*

# ABCDEFGHIJKLM NOPQRSTUVWXYZ abcdefghijklmn opqrstuvwxyz

# ABCDEFGHIJKLM NOPQRSTUVWXYZ abcdefghijklm nopqrstuvwxyz

Opposite: The first issue of the ITC magazine *U&lc*, 1973. Designed by Herb Lubalin, it contained a blistering attack on type piracy – an issue that was to become increasingly important as type broke away from being the proprietary design with a particular system. Copying was an irritating, parasitic problem in the photocomposition era, but this would become pandemic with the ease of duplication made possible by digital information technology of the late 1980s onwards. Early ITC faces – shown here Souvenir (Ed Benguiat, 1970), American Typewriter (design by Joel Kaden and Tony Stan, 1974), Serif Gothic (Herb Lubalin and Tony DiSpagna, 1972-4) – tended to an exaggerated x-height and a narrow body, the compacted, close-set appearance being a look that became associated with the decade almost as much as tight flared trousers and large collars. Right: Strong designs carried on the promotional brochures used to launch ITC faces.

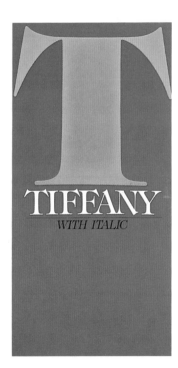

glass negative image of the font, was remarkable for its sharpness and accuracy of output.

The process of drawing type began to undergo significant change with the arrival of on-screen computer-aided design. To the fore was the Ikarus system developed by Peter Karow in Hamburg. Launched in 1974, it was adopted by Berthold and Linotype and soon found users across Europe, the US and in Japan. It offered a way of converting screen-designed images to line drawings; converting drawings to digitized information for screen working, and a way of automatically developing variants around the key design, so assisting production of a comprehensive type family. Other systems were launched with comparable facilities, but updated forms of Ikarus remained the most widely employed at the top end of

type-design programs into the 1990s, although in the late 1980s Fontographer emerged as the most commonly used program on the personal computer.

Besides the changing methods, the meaning of design was also shifting. After almost two decades of the International Style gaining strength, its beliefs were now seriously questioned. The key reaction started in its homeland, with ideas that were later seen as the New Wave. The key instigator was Swiss designer Wolfgang Weingart (1941–).

In 1968 Weingart began working at the Basel School of Design, whose teaching he had rejected as a student in opposition to the dogmatic approach identified with the Swiss typography of Emil Ruder and Armin Hofmann, both

Left: from a special edition of *Typografische Monatsblätter*, December 1976, designed by and featuring the work and writings of Wolfgang Weingart. Broken and cut grids, reversed and stepped blocks, different ranging points for text – such devices and more became part of Weingart's mannered response to the dominance of Swiss Style reduction. Weingart's search to revive expression gave birth to the New Wave typography and became an important influence in the US. Under the provocative pyrotechnics with type that his imitators made into mere style, Weingart was investigating the potential of changing media. Opposite: in *Typografische Monatsblätter* 12, 1972, a special section on education co-edited by Weingart featured studies by his colleague at Basle, Peter von Arx, who argued "the prospective designer should become familiar with the factors of movement, time and speed" as seen in film.

on the staff. But their recognition of his talents led to an invitation to come back and present an alternative voice. In so doing he placed himself at the centre of a new orthodoxy and circle of influence that stretched across Europe to the West Coast of the US (Dan Friedman and April Greiman being his most noted followers).

Weingart rejected the reductive approach that had taken Swiss typography to its position of pre-eminent intellectual credibility. Where Josef Müller-Brockmann reduced type to one face in two sizes (text and headline) positioned in a clear relationship and organized around the right angle and placed on a grid, Weingart asked his class to find principles of typographic composition that did not rely on any systematic approach, but drew from the structures suggested by the

production processes of the piece itself. He wanted typographic design mixed in as part of a range of tools within the graphic designer's control. His students studied other areas such as photography, drawing, colour theory and packaging.

From this dedication to the potential of the tools and their expressive qualities emerged an introspective form of design in keeping with the mood of an era. Self-conscious forms were apparent in metafictional literature and films, and music that questioned music structure. This trend was followed by three-dimensional design (with works by the Memphis group in the early 1980s) and postmodern architecture.

Such radicalism soon became formulaic. Weingart has admitted that the experimentation he sought to foster, and which is apparent in his own work, was inspired by the potential of pushing hot-metal processes to the limit and standing them on their head. This led to stylized features – stepped blocks, bold reversal out of type, varying letter spacing and underlining, to name but a few tropes – becoming associated with the "New Wave" typographers. A common visual emphasis would be heavily screened photography with the halftone dot size visible so that the picture self-consciously displays its method of illusion.

The Swiss origins are still there. Weingart favoured certain families and tended to stick with them, his preferred faces being Akzidenz Grotesk, Helvetica and Univers of the sans serifs (mostly used for the poster and other display work emanating from his class and studio) and Times and

Left: 1971 poster by A. G. Fronzoni (born 1923). This Italian Minimalist probed the boundaries of type size, of print colour, of the edge of the medium, and to what reduction characters could be taken while still being readable. Below: Frutiger, designed by Adrian Frutiger, 1973-6. Created for signage at Charles de Gaulle Airport, Paris, it was issued by Linotype in 1976. A descendant of Univers, it is more open (note the "c" and the "e") with small capitals and longer ascenders and descenders. Frutiger looked back to Roman capitals and away from geometric sans. Opposite top: Bell Centennial, 1975-8, and Galliard, 1978, by Matthew Carter for Linotype. The first was commissioned by AT&T as a directory face to fit more into less space. Carter designed forms that retain distinctions even when degraded. The exaggerated cut-aways in small sizes allow for inkspread. Galliard was a revival of a sixteenth-century design by Robert Granjon, more true to Garamond than the many other revivals. Opposite: pictograms by Otl Aicher for the Munich Olympics, 1972, based on a 20x20 grid, a key contribution to the international language of non-text marks. Far right: Mobil identity newsletter, from 1975, design by Chermayeff & Geismar Associates, spreading the culture of global typography.

Frutiger *18pt*

ABCDEFGHIJKLMNOPQRSTUVWXYZ
abcdefghijklmnopqrstuvwxyz

ABCDEFGHIJKLM
NOPQRSTUVWXYZ
abcdefghijklm
nopqrstuvwxyz

ABCDEFGHIJKLM
NOPQRSTUVWXYZ
abcdefghijklm
nopqrstuvwxyz

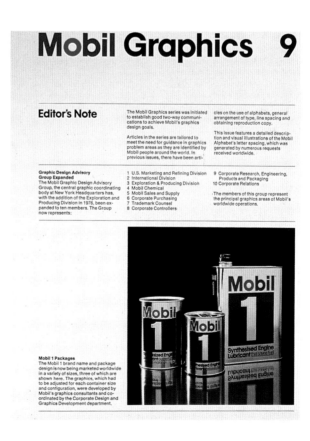

# Mobil Graphics 9

### Editor's Note

The Mobil Graphics series was initiated to establish good two-way communications to achieve Mobil's graphics design goals.

Articles in the series are tailored to meet the need for guidance in graphics problem areas as they are identified by Mobil people around the world. In previous issues, there have been arti-

cles on the use of alphabets, general arrangement of type, line spacing and obtaining reproduction copy.

This issue features a detailed description and visual illustrations of the Mobil Alphabet's letter spacing, which was generated by numerous requests received worldwide.

**Graphic Design Advisory Group Expanded**
The Mobil Graphic Design Advisory Group, the central graphic coordinating body at New York Headquarters has, with the addition of the Exploration and Producing Division in 1976, been expanded to ten members. The Group now represents:

1 U.S. Marketing and Refining Division
2 International Division
3 Exploration & Producing Division
4 Mobil Chemical
5 Mobil Sales and Supply
6 Corporate Purchasing
7 Trademark Counsel
8 Corporate Controllers

9 Corporate Research, Engineering, Products and Packaging
10 Corporate Relations

The members of this group represent the principal graphics areas of Mobil's worldwide operations.

**Mobil 1 Packages**
The Mobil 1 brand name and package design is now being marketed worldwide in a variety of sizes, three of which are shown here. The graphics, which had to be adjusted for each container size and configuration, were developed by Mobil's graphics consultants and coordinated by the Corporate Design and Graphics Development department.

Garamond (for text). Weingart's aim was to break free of the "stiff and boring" orthodoxy that he felt slavish adherence to Swiss Style had led typography into: although his direct influence has been to create a new style, New Wave, the thrust of his teaching was actually anti-style.

Reaction and rejection of a different order was apparent in the style of graphics associated with the punk and new music scene of the late 1970s. Here, again, the music industry showed it had the ephemeral, inquisitive, novelty-seeking nature to throw up challenges. The work of young designers in the UK, the main ground for the short-lived movement, stands out. Designers like Barney Bubbles (Colin Fulcher), Jamie Reid, Malcolm Garrett and Peter Saville launched their reputations, not by creating a prevailing aesthetic, but by a

wave of invention, of pillaging history and vernacular without excessive respect. Like the music they were packaging, they celebrated the idea that their medium was more about emotion in communication than reason.

Right: the extremes of the 1970s: the International Style rules of control even extended to this self-conscious range of "Basics" packaging from Sainsbury supermarkets in Britain in the early 1970s. The own-brand products were colour-coded with mostly sans serif typefaces and minimal graphic elements to suggest good value. In contrast, establishment values of all kinds were under attack by punk graphics, opposite right, which were like the music in determinedly kicking at conventions. Leading the charge were Jamie Reid's covers for the Sex Pistols, here the back of the 1977 album *Never Mind The Bollocks*. Its "ransom note" style typography was part of a general strategy of appropriation and subversion, ideas taken in part from the 1960s Situationist movement. Opposite left: somewhere in between, the experimental could also be seen in the convergence of graphics and film with computer effects. The movie titles of R/Greenberg Associates in the late 1970s were among the first to use super-computers to to drive out graphic effects on sequences for *Alien* (as here) and *Superman*, both big budget spectaculars. This was part of the groundwork for tools that would become commonplace in computer manipulation.

"Most of my life," recalled Matthew Carter in the late 1980s, "I dreaded situations like dinner parties where people ask you what you do for a living. People had no idea what a type designer actually did. Nowadays I'll be in a restaurant and a waiter will come up to me and ask, 'Did I hear you talking about fonts?'"[1]

An exceptional waiter, perhaps, but such was the radical shift in the access to typographic decision-making in the 1980s. From being an arcane area that many graphic designers had only elementary knowledge of, typography was, by the end of the decade, being practised in millions of homes and offices.

This was due to the arrival of the personal computer. The PC was launched by IBM in the early 1980s and became widely "cloned", in other words, copied by much cheaper rival products being sold that were capable of running the same software. No longer did users need a degree in computer science to operate such a machine, and users could afford to buy the tools to add functions to their computer. This separation of the functionality of software from hardware was a development that underpinned the new form of type design and layout. Typographic control was no longer related to the use of large systems, as with hot metal or photosetting.

The launch of the Apple Macintosh personal computer in 1984 set the pace for developing user-friendly systems: it featured wysiwyg presentation ("what you see is what you get"), not only for showing text but for simulating the wider creative working environment. This made possible the practice of "desktop publishing", a much-used phrase applied to the potential given by the new systems for creating and outputting publishable material, either in finished form (via a desktop printer) or ready to give to an external printer. Typesetting and other print-room skills were merged into the same process as that required for designing on-screen. Designers began to do their own typesetting. Software layout packages, such as PageMaker and QuarkXPress, simulated the graphic designer's work tools and desk on-screen. Initially crude in their typographic sensitivity, these packages were rapidly upgraded in response to both user demand and to take up the benefits of the fast-advancing technology.

Besides the transfer of fonts to the digital environment, and the growth of font vendors in this environment (see Bitstream and Emigre below), the fact that type choice, however crude, was commonly available on-screen, created a new perception of this subject. The "Mac" came bundled with a clutch of fonts as part of its system software: these included versions of Courier (a backwards reference to the typewriter), Helvetica and Times, and also new screen fonts that worked at the low-resolution (72 dots per inch) of on-screen display – Chicago (used on the system display itself), Geneva, Monaco and New York. They were not for printing, but existed only for the on-screen world.

The "Mac" and related software were by the end of the decade developed to such an extent that the graphics

industry was switching over rapidly to the control, speed and economy it made possible. Diverse software for handling the input of words and pictures into the on-screen layout was produced, increasingly releasing functions only half-dreamed of pre-digitally. To some degree the new processes were driving the graphics (a simple example of this would be that the default settings and screen display suggestions within a program would encourage designers to take up certain options). In other words, decisions were constructed around the parameters laid down by the program writers. Lower-cost scanners and easier links with other programs provided the means for integrating the computer with the mass of other print, photographic and film information that a designer may need to draw on. At the same time developments in software for related areas of activity, notably word processing, supported the transfer of the material handled by typographers into the new technology. For the first time there existed a seamless production process in which all the material could be generated in the same format – digitally – and pulled together in one creative production centre, the desktop computer environment.

This did not happen overnight, but nearly. Into the early 1990s the majority of print production took place with traditional methods heavily involved. But the rapid adoption and development of the technology happened at a pace much faster than the move to previous technologies in print and communications. Where hot metal took decades to become established and gain the support of a wide variety of typefaces, and photosetting took twenty years to turn around from initial take-up to dominance, the digital revolution prevailed within a decade. From virtually zero computing in design at the start of the 1980s, by 1990 a survey in the US reported that 68 per cent of graphic designers used computers and a further 26 per cent were in the process of buying a system.[2]

"Within my experience, the time taken to conceptualize and produce a real letter character has gone from a year to a day," Matthew Carter commented, contrasting the beginnings of his type design career (learning punchcutting at the venerable Dutch printing firm Enschedé in the 1950s) with the power that off-the-shelf font design programs gave designers by the mid-to-late 1980s.[3] Carter's career neatly encapsulated the changes. After working for Crosfield and then Linotype as a designer who adapted and developed types for photocomposition, he formed Bitstream in 1981, with colleagues from Linotype. To a degree it followed the route mapped out by the International Typeface Corporation, that of a system-independent type supplier. Bitstream sold digitized typefaces to the new companies that were launching electronic imaging equipment and needed type libraries to make their systems viable. Rather than each individual manufacturer having to develop libraries, Bitstream launched a rapid programme of digital face development and licensed the faces. Many of the classic faces had to be incorporated to offer a useful library, and so the great majority of Bitstream faces are those whose basic forms are in the public domain or are licensed from others. Over the decade the library grew to more than a thousand faces, which were

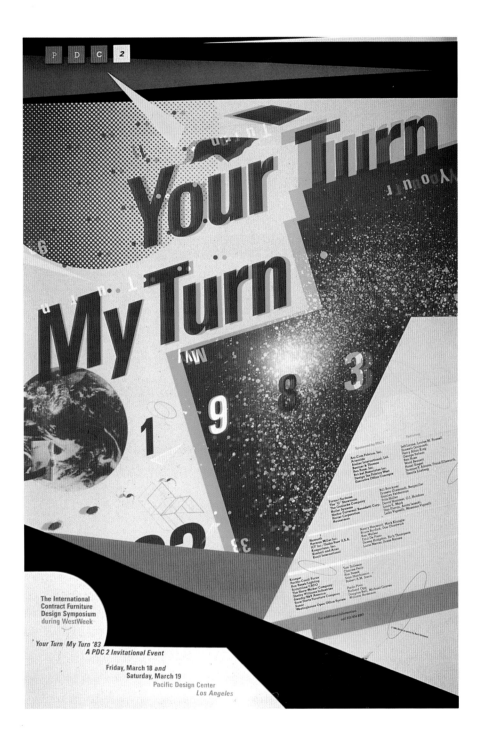

Left: poster by April Greiman for the Pacific Design Center, 1983. From the basis of studies under Wolfgang Weingart in the 1970s, Greiman (born 1948) developed her own West Coast spin on these ideas, forming an approach she dubbed "hybrid imagery", which drew on the language of video and computer as well as print graphics. The self-consciousness of the work is to the fore, with suggestions of colour registration, of the dot of half-tone screen, and cutting away at the printed plane. At the same time there is a degree of rigour to the ordering of the various blocks of information that harks back to the Swiss Style.

licensed to around three hundred manufacturers – an indication of the explosion in options available for outputting type, when compared to the small group of manufacturers seriously able to invest in hot metal and then photocomposition technology.

The library includes important new designs, beginning with Carter's own Charter (1987). This was one of a number of faces designed to tackle the challenge of variable printer quality and how it could degrade a face. With a high-resolution typesetter, 1200 dpi (dots per inch) or more, the finer points of a design will be reproduced. But with the 300 dpi printers (and some even lower resolution) that were common, many faces broke up. This was an acute problem in smaller sizes where the number of dots drawing the design

of, say, an eight-point character, would be insufficient to render fine serifs. Charter responded to these conditions by offering a limited family (regular, bold, black and italic) that had sturdy, open letterforms, that do not lose definition or fill in when produced on standard low-resolution printers.

Early ground rules for coping with low-resolution output were presented in Gerard Unger's family of faces (Demos, Praxis and Flora), released between 1976 and 1980 while he was working with the pioneering German digital typesetting manufacturer Dr. Ing. Rudolf Hell GmbH. The three, respectively, serif, sans serif and italic forms, demonstrated the large x-height, openness and sturdiness seen in the later Amerigo, Charter and other digital faces intended for wide-ranging application. Unger noted that the requirements of

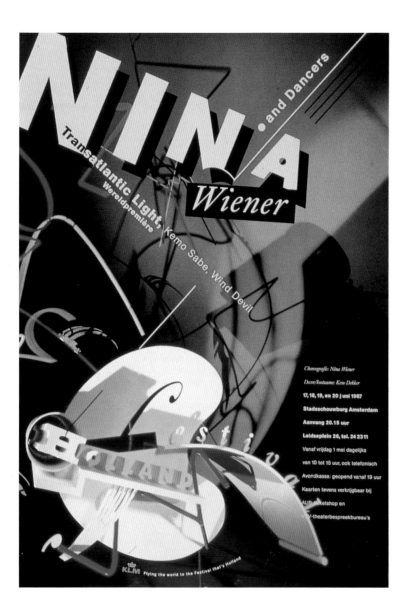

Opposite: Lucida, designed by Charles Bigelow and Kris Holmes for Adobe in 1985, was the first original face designed for laser printers, being tolerant of different resolutions of output. Stone Sans was part of an 18-font family designed in 1984–7 by Sumner Stone for Adobe which was intended to work on digital technology for anything from low-resolution display advertising through to fine text in books. Left: in the mid to late 1980s Studio Dumbar in The Hague was at the forefront of a wave of influential design coming out of The Netherlands. Led by Gert Dumbar (born 1941), who built on the Dutch Modernists such as Piet Zwart, the studio often used constructions that mixed flat art with staged photography, playing with the viewer's perspective.

these faces was not so dissimilar to the basic parameters of effective, straightforward typeface design of the last four hundred years.

Kris Holmes and Charles Bigelow's Lucida family (1985) for Adobe Systems (which had a type-design programme in support of its graphic design-related software products) took this idea further, drawing on legibility and readability research to develop a simplified sans serif and serif that would reproduce the preferred characteristics of classic typefaces but through the terms of the new low-resolution technology, rather than against it. Holmes explained that:

"The basic Lucida letterforms are purposely free of complexity and fussiness so that the underlying letter shapes can emerge legibly from the 'noise' of the printer-marking techniques. Certain traditionally complex details, such as swelling stems, brackets, and serifs are rendered diagrammatically as polygonal shapes rather than as subtle curves. In small sizes and low resolutions, these produce clear forms; in larger sizes and higher resolutions, they reveal interesting modulations."

Holmes and Bigelow created a comparable range of bitmapped screen fonts called Pellucida, conceived to best express the different qualities of the family on the poor resolution of the monitor (72 dpi equivalent on a typical display). All faces for digital setting need to have a screen font version, but the inaccuracy of many made them difficult to work with as what you saw was not what you got.

**Lucida** *30pt*

A B C D E F G H I J K L M
N O P Q R S T U V W X Y Z
a b c d e f g h i j k l m n o p
q r s t u v w x y z

**Stone Sans** *30pt*

A B C D E F G H I J K L M
N O P Q R S T U V W X Y Z
a b c d e f g h i j k l m n o p
q r s t u v w x y z

A problem with screen fonts, besides their low resolution, was that they were often partly drawn by the computer from knowledge of the nearest sizes: this can lead to highly unattractive renditions of the face on screen as the computer may "refine" the wrong elements of the design. Adobe, the company behind Lucida, pioneered a method called "hinting" to overcome this drawback. This process builds information into the type that automatically adjusts the face in small sizes to combat low-resolution problems, putting in elements to retain characteristics, but it does so at the cost of some of the original character of the design. However, with the launch of its program Adobe Type Manager the company delivered an industry-standard technology that removed the troublesome "bitmapping" effect of enlarging fonts beyond the size at which they were originally constructed. The

proliferation of digital software and hardware also created a demand for a common language for type information in computer files. Different languages were developed, but the victory went to Adobe's PostScript, launched in 1983. Rather than working with a bitmapped image, PostScript draws and fills in Bezier curves to achieve a better print image.

While many designers could – and did – go on producing work that looked pretty much as it would have using photosetting or even hot metal, a new generation of designers picked up on the freedom with which typographical form could now be exploited, aided and abetted by other media technology advances in photographic and film form.

The West Coast magazine *Emigre* was important as both a demonstration of new ideas and a rallying point for debate on digital type and design-related issues. Initially an attempt at a lifestyle magazine when launched in 1984, it moved increasingly to being a design, then a typographic, magazine. This was related to the growth of the digital font business of *Emigre* founders Rudy VanderLans and Zuzana Licko. With Licko as chief designer and other designers' faces included in their distribution, their fonts began with raw explorations of the bitmap structure and moved on to address aesthetic issues that responded closely to the potential of the systems and the concerns of the design community.

A highy influential figure in this period was Neville Brody, whose work on the British style magazines *The Face* and

*Arena* became internationally known – an effect propagated by the growth of general media interest in fashionable graphics, along with the publication in 1988 of a book, *The Graphic Language of Neville Brody*, and a world-touring exhibition. Such a phenomenon was, arguably, a result of the new generation of graphic producers enfranchised by digital technology: now typography was not remote, graphic style was more accessible – almost like fashion or food, just one more aspect of taste to understand and explore.

Crudely measured, the results of the "Brody school" could be seen in the exploitation of letterforms as graphic devices, the do-it-yourself design of new display forms (Brody drew the Constructivist-influenced typefaces he used on *The Face* by hand, but they have an aesthetic that relates to the bitmap

Industria Solid *21pt*

ABCDEFGHIJKLMNOPQRSTUVWXYZ
abcdefghijklmnopqrstuvwxyz

Insignia *21pt*

ABCDEFGHIJKLM
NOPQRSTUVWXYZ
abcdefghijklmnop
qrstuvwxyz

Opposite: after Neville Brody built his reputation, Brody-like typography was commonplace – this advertisement is one of the few he designed, rather than being a pastiche of his work. Above: two of his early pre-digital typefaces. Right: record sleeve by Vaughan Oliver, 1988 – florid type and dark imagery were trademarks in his influential output for 4AD records.

fonts) and in the reliance on typographic elements as expressive features of the page. In its picking up of the language of digital typography as something to exploit and express, there were connections, albeit unspoken, with the New Wave approach of expressionist typography taught by Wolfgang Weingart.

Another designer involved in the influential batch of "style magazines" of the 1980s was Terry Jones, who launched *i-D* magazine. Here legibility was questioned in a manner akin to the psychedelia of the late 1960s, with text subverted by garish overprinting and crude typewriter text, copy reversed out from four colour, photocopier distortions added and many more graphic experiments thrown into the pot besides. All this "noise" was part of the message, of course. For the

audience of *i-D*, typographic quality involved view-ability as much as legibility in creating readability. Style magazines such as *i-D*, *The Face* and *Blitz* in England, or related magazines such as *Actuel* in France or *Wiener* in Germany, were badges of affiliation to be worn as well as to read.

Teaching practice was falling a generation behind what was happening around new technology and the style magazine typography. With colleges and their staff largely wedded to older technology and teaching programmes related thereto, they had difficulty, both conceptually and economically, in embracing the latest equipment as freely as had ambitious studios or publishing operations. But one school that did make its mark was the Cranbrook Academy of Art in the US, where the postgraduate teaching and work of Katherine

**Matrix** *21pt*

ABCDEFGHIJKLMN
OPQRSTUVWXYZ
abcdefghijklmnop
qrstuvwxyz

Above and opposite: examples of the early output of Emigre Graphics, the company set up by Rudy VanderLans and Zuzana Licko in 1984. Beginning with the early Macintosh as the design tool, Licko produced a range of bitmapped fonts, such as Emigre Eight, in the mid-1980s. Her designs developed with the technology; Matrix, above, shows an attempt to create a face with serifs that would be extremely robust for low-resolution output. Left: questioning Modernism, American designers were exploring their vernacular as a rich source of typography – and Tibor Kalman (born 1949) was among the most witty, as with this menu for an up-scale diner which takes the letter board of a down-scale diner, but introduces Apollinaire-like typographic puns. Opposite right: New Order Confusion cover, 1983, by Peter Saville, a pioneer of typographic cool.

McCoy in graphics during the 1980s, supported by key students such as Jeffery Keedy, Edward Fella, Scott Makela, David Frej and Allen Hori, was to have an influence beyond its small academic environment. In the following years its students would feed out to head up many of the leading graphics courses in the States. McCoy's direction can be seen in an early pre-digital project with the design of an issue of the academic communication theory magazine *Visible Language* in 1978, where the text was deconstructed by a variety of typographic devices (such as reversals, hugely exaggerated word spacing and ragged margins, all showing the influence of Weingart). McCoy explored the "linguistics" of typography, seeking to isolate the "hardware" – the basic structure of the communication – from the "software" – the meaning in the work. The dislocation sought to prise loose

**Emigre Eight** *42pt*

# ABCDEFGHIJKLMNOPQRSTUVWXYZ
# abcdefghijklmnopqrstuvwxyz

an awareness of the signified from the signifier, to use the terminology found in the writings of a Cranbrook influence, pioneering language theoretician Ferdinand de Saussure (the notoriously long reading list of the school drew heavily on structuralist and deconstructionist thinkers). While most of the work did not depend on new technology for its execution, in its diversity and intellectual drive, the Cranbrook Academy sought to present a new agenda for typography. Not entirely coincidentally, there was an emerging technology ready to help this happen.

In televisual graphics, new systems fostered new techniques during the 1980s – notably the image-manipulation and retouching machines pioneered by Quantel (Paintbox and, later, Harry) that offered a powerful method of manipulating

frame-by-frame movement, integrating graphic effects and live action. But there was still little effort applied to generating new faces specially created for the unique conditions of television, despite this being the prime medium of communication. Type would tend to be a bold face with crudely spaced and leaded lines ("TV spacing", as it was commonly known), or there would be an attempt at something more adventurous that would fall foul of the unsuitable nature of print faces on screen. Fine weights and serif forms do not survive the 625-line-or-less boiling mass of information supplied by the rolling scan of television image-construction.

Besides the innovation in technology and the work of those designers attuned to it, there were eclectic revivals and

The 1980s threw up questions that bypassed type design history, with the "transparency" of type and its fine history in metal becoming increasingly redundant in electronic media. Opposite top: The time-based dot matrix of indicator boards (as with the London Underground signage introduced in the late 1980s) demands viewer participation and awareness of the moment of the message. This has prompted art works such as Jenny Holzer's piece from 1988, a slogan in Spectacolor above Piccadilly Circus, right. Such conceptual pieces of typographic-based art have probed the relationship between text, image and viewer, bringing an awareness of dimensions beyond the print tradition of type. Opposite: The dislike of Chicago in the typographic establishment has no effect on its prevalence or strong functionality as the default font on several generations of Macintosh computers, and representing the operating system. Chicago is one of the original "city" fonts supplied with the Macintosh in 1984, designs intended for high legibility on a 72dpi screen and not for print.

Chicago *48pt*

 File   Edit   View   Label   Special

# ABCDEFGHIJKLM
# NOPQRSTUVWXYZ
# abcdefghijklmn
# opqrstuvwxyz

cross-fertilizations of graphics. This was aided by the ease with which scanners made it possible to suck material into a computer layout. Typographers could take old faces that may exist only in a specimen book or a piece of print and scan and rework them to create either one image or a new font. Computers had shifted the very nature of graphics: all was now data, and the "remix" process in design was entering a new era.

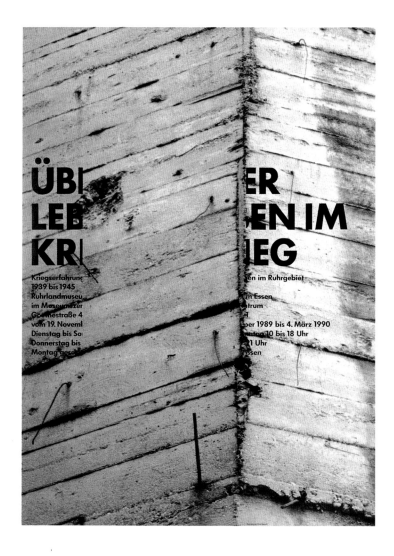

Opposite left: in 1986 the journal
Octavo was launched by a group
of designers in London called
8vo who were dedicated to
arguing a Modernist case for
higher quality in typography and
against the "mediocrity" that
they saw around them. Simon
Johnston, Mark Holt, Michael
Burke and Hamish Muir set out
to publish eight, 16-page issues,
which took them until 1992, by
which time Johnston had left.
Despite having only a small
circulation, the journal was a
marker for retaining the spirit of
the Modernist pioneers.
Opposite right: the European
cultural poster tradition was
the refuge of many leading
designers. In Germany, Uwe
Loesch (born 1943) combined
minimal messages (this poster
headline reads "Survival during
war") with concept-based layout.
Right: titles for a UK television
programme, 1988, by English
Markell & Pockett. New post-
production systems were
allowing designers to incorporate
type into dramatic film and video
effects. Here the words streamed
in projections on faces and in
abstraction before spooling into
the words of the programme title.

1990

A postcard issued in 1996 promoting the new typeface FF Schmalhans by Hans Reichel proclaimed itself as "the 3 million 285 thousand 467th font ever to be made in the Universe". It proposed that the universe could take up to four million fonts, so there was room enough for a newcomer. While the first figure was an exaggeration, the second figure was an underestimation of the infinite variety of fonts now possible. Reichel's little joke addressed the incredible proliferation of type design in the 1990s, a boom that blew apart the assumptions of what type involved. With a technology that allowed anyone with a personal computer to draw or customize their own typeface, or at least pick'n'mix an assorted font, the total user base of PCs suggested that a community in excess of one hundred million typographers and type designers existed by the late 1990s. This contrasted with the tens of thousands of type specifiers (such as designers, art directors and printers) in previous generations, and the few hundred people at most who actually designed type in the days of hot metal.

Of course, most PC users did not (and do not) design or even play with type beyond perhaps changing the default font, using the bold and italic options, or increasing the type size and leading. And yet they work with letterforms and typographic controls in a way that never existed for the end user before the digital era. The PC brought together functions previously carried out by handwriting, the typewriter and professional typesetting. It took typography to the layperson – even if they did not necessarily want the responsibility that goes with the power; if they did not actively think of typography, their computer would be doing it for them, producing typographic matter "on the fly" as it generated text or downloaded internet pages with a default font crudely "setting" the requested information.

Even within the professional design community, the quantity of new type design in the 1990s was unprecedented – to a scale that makes estimating the number of typefaces in circulation almost impossible. While the major type vendors rapidly moved their large libraries to digital form and on to searchable CD-Roms offering thousands of fonts – buying in new designs and marketing the libraries widely, often with cross-distribution of each others' fonts – their once dominant activities were increasingly meeting hot competition from the explosion of small font companies and independent designers.

Emigre showed that type "brands" could be launched out of the new technology. By the early 1990s, Emigre had become a byword for experimental fonts, to the point that a 1993 issue of the influential music magazine *Ray Gun* proclaimed on the cover "No Emigre fonts" as a signal from the leading art director David Carson (see below) that he was not dependent on the company's designs for creative expression. Emigre traded its type at the premium end of the market, with a small list of unusual fonts offered at a high price, in contrast to the "pile 'em high, sell 'em cheap" tendencies of larger companies. It was wedded to a policy where each design seemed as much a theoretical statement about the potential of type as it was a functional font.

Emigre's flirting with music publishing suggested the model of the business, which was more like a small record label in its brand image and business strategy, seeming to rely on the odd hit typeface for survival. Template Gothic by Barry Deck (1990) was for a while a highly popular Emigre-distributed face that came to signal the Zeitgeist to the point that design magazines proclaimed it (somewhat prematurely) "typeface of the decade". Through stencil-like structures seemingly unlinked to written forms, it combined the vernacular (Laundromat signage) with a suggestion of new technology – hi-fi brands and telephone companies found it perfect for styling their ads.

By late 1997 the Emigre catalogue featured around two hundred faces, with the "house" designer Zuzana Licko as the key contributor. By this point, Licko and Rudy VanderLans (the publisher/editor of *Emigre* magazine) had pursued their path long enough and with sufficient purity of purpose to earn themselves a retrospective at the San Francisco Museum of Modern Art.

FontShop International was a more commercially motivated type design business, also owing its existence to the digital revolution. Founded in 1990 by the graphic designers/type designers Neville Brody in London and Erik Spiekermann in Berlin, it has been no less experimental in the nature of the typefaces it publishes and distributes, but has grown much faster than Emigre thanks to a stronger system of franchise distributors. By the end of 1997, FSI had a library of more than one thousand faces, with a type catalogue that needed updating quarterly in order to take in the new launches. Faces (such as Schmalhans, above) were branded under the FontFont "label" with "FF" appended to the name. More than eighty designers were represented.

FSI worked through a network of distributors covering various parts of the world, although it had problems with the management and control of some of these, notably in the US and UK. At one point in 1996, Brody, as represented in FSI, was taking legal action against his UK distributor FontWorks, where he had 51 per cent ownership, which was threatening a counteraction against FSI. This problem led to FSI partnering with Monotype as a new distributor of its fonts, bringing together one of the old major "labels" in type design with the new force.

FSI successfully focused on building its brand around innovative contemporary type design. Once again, the music or book business comes to mind, rather than the old practices of type companies: instead of having an in-house studio as the main engine of the latest faces, FSI worked as a publisher whose reputation drew in new designers and new designs from existing designers. The "cool" credential of its founders combined with the energetic marketing of its distributors (who also brought in new fonts and designers) to make a highly competitive operation unburdened by any pre-digital history or other business activity.

Typefaces were no longer being sold off the back of some proprietary system, as with hot metal or photosetting, nor

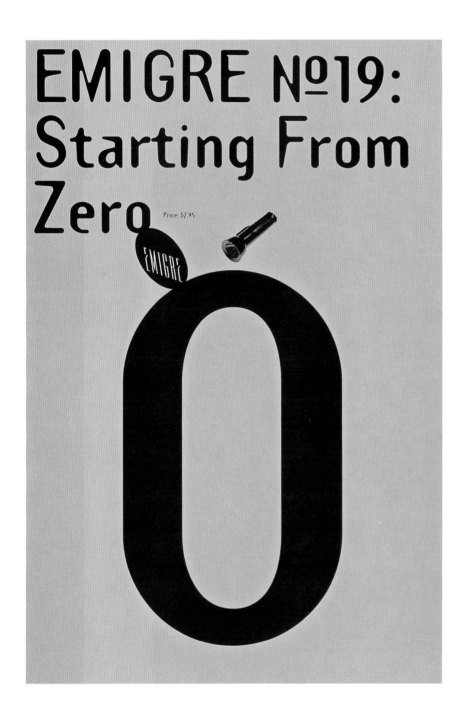

With Emigre's "Starting From Zero" issue of 1991, the face Template Gothic gained its first official airing. Designed by Barry Deck and distributed by Emigre, it was quickly called "typeface of the decade" by one magazine and it became highly fashionable. While the aesthetic is derived from Laundromat signage, the characters suggested screen-derived forms – an association to please a culture in which the computer had at last become "personal", and a friendly tool to use at work, rest and play.

was there the wholesale digitizing of familiar faces as with Bitstream. Instead, in the 1990s the emphasis became less on working within a technology (a photosetting or hot-metal system, or even a Letraset sheet) and more purely on the creative content being marketed. While being by no means the leading distributors of fonts in total, there has been a pioneering nature to the activities of FSI and Emigre around which a whole new industry of type companies and type design practice has emerged. Small foundries such as [T-26] or House Industries, or the designer/distributors such as Jon Barnbrook with his Virus label or Jean-François Porchez's Typofonderie, are only able to create and distribute fonts because of digital technology. FontNet, an offshoot of the British distributor FontWorks, was set up to provide an internet hub for such small labels to work through.

Although all was rapidly becoming digital, issues such as the choice of computer platform (PC or Mac) or type format (PostScript or TrueType fonts) could still cloud the picture. Fonts tended to be released to cover all profitable eventualities, as the adaptations required software tweakings rather than any investment bound up in a physical product. The wave of new companies also worked as a further spur to the rejuvenation of more traditional type developers and distributors. However, they already had the motivation to get out of the fast-failing old technology where type was attached to proprietary systems.

The death and rebirth of Monotype illustrates this pattern: after some years of restructuring, matters came to a head at the Monotype Corporation in 1992 when the business was put into receivership. This was after an awkward period of shifting ownership, but the key problem was the speed of change to desktop publishing and the dying market for old typesetting systems. Out of this was born a new company, Monotype Typography, a software-based company which went on to celebrate its centenary of "type making" in 1997 on the back of a business built on realizing the value of the archive of classic fonts, along with custom design and consultancy work. The shift to living by intellectual property had started to happen before the liquidation, with font licensing deals struck with Apple Computer in 1989 and Microsoft from 1990. In 1990 the company issued a CD-Rom of its entire "classics" collection, along with the Adobe Type Library. The Adobe Type Library had rapidly grown to be a major typographic presence, helped by Adobe's dominance in providing the PostScript technology of type description. By 1998, the Monotype double-CD pack featured around five thousand typefaces and was not only marketing the Adobe and FSI libraries, but had launched The Creative Alliance with Agfa, a brand name aimed at combining their substantial main brand reputations while declaring an interest in innovation (with a cluster of innovative typefaces and designers brought in for support).

Linotype and Berthold were other major traditional typesetting system companies that had a difficult passage in the 1990s as they fought to realign their businesses and to realize the value of their intellectual assets against the decline of their traditional business. In contrast, the purely software-based Adobe rapidly grew to having one of the largest and best distributed type libraries, being in the useful position of controlling the use of the PostScript standard which had emerged as the standard font description software. This gave Adobe considerable room for leverage when it came to developing and licensing type.

CD-Roms and catalogues were generally distributed free and in increasingly vast numbers during the 1990s. A phone call was all it would then take to unlock a typeface on the disk, or to download it over the telephone line, or to have it shipped across town or for next day delivery. Considerable creative and physical costs were often invested in the packaging: the work of Carlos Segura and his [T-26] presentation packages is an example of the baroque extremes reached: typefaces were packaged in cute burlap sacks containing a host of printed sample material, while QuickTime movies were made to demonstrate the moving qualities of the type. [T-26] fonts have an air of physicality that belies the fact that the core products are invisible bits of information.

The internet emerged as a means for promoting and distributing a font without requiring physical packaging or a distribution medium. This worked for commercial type companies, and also for the hacker world of computer activity. Many fonts were (and are) placed on the web for free or "shareware" distribution but, inevitably, these efforts are less than complete in their character sets, functionality or quality. Often they display more than a little plagiarizing, with software such as the leading type design package Fontographer making it relatively easy to take in character forms, adapt them and re-name them as something new. Even less honourable was the practice of illicit internet offerings of whole libraries of copyrighted fonts (along with other software), downloaded for free. It is also common in major cities to have illegal operators of software downloads, who for a price will turn up and copy a whole archive of material on to a computer hard drive.

Such activities realized the darkest fears of the type publishing community, who faced not only deliberate copyright infringement, but also confusion as to what was and was not permissible in the carrying and transferring of fonts. For designers and publishers, the need to buy a typeface not only for their own creative use but for the company which might carry out the subsequent imagesetting proved an unpalatable increase to their costs, which often prompted them to give a copy of the font to the output company. Against this software, developers have worked to raise awareness about copyright law, devise controls restricting digital copying (so far largely unsuccessfully) and have lobbied for stronger action to curb illegal copying (in particular, the lack of recognition of type design factors in law, rather than patents on names, has been a problem in bringing actions in the United States). Developers argued that digital technology could undermine the basis for serious type development. When the product of years of work can be copied perfectly in a few seconds and then used without charge, there is seemingly little incentive to make a business out of high quality type design.

It became apparent that an important development, particularly with regard to the internet, would be the creation of a technology that allowed the viewing of a typeface without permitting the user to create with it or take it elsewhere. The OpenType standard being developed for the internet enables the user to embed type design code within web pages, delivering accurate images of the particular characters without having to download and hold the particular fonts used on each and every user's computer.

This radical shifting in technology and rapid change and growth in the marketing of type was motivated by a new use and appreciation of the actual artefacts of type and typography. In the 1990s we had it all. As ever, our typography reflected society's deepest concerns, but rarely in a way that was ever made as a conscious, collective effort. Instead, we had every remembered form of graphic design from the past recycled as style – in almost any country in the world you could pass from pseudo-traditional lettering on food packaging to techno pop music typography, to some minimalist setting of words in fashion advertising. Type was a signifier of the diversity possible in a world that had largely capitulated to the power of the capitalist model of production – where choice, or the illusion thereof, is seen as a right. Now typography aimed to clothe, rather than transparently communicate (the sometime innocent purpose of typographers past).

Any cynicism about the marketing-led values of most typographic production should not obscure the real climate for radical innovation in these years, though. The maturing of advances in computers and in global media delivered a new

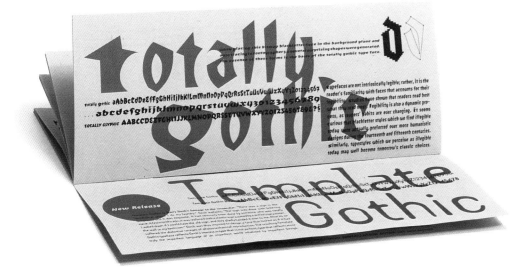

Left: Emigre's fonts in the 1990s became increasingly varied – from technology-centred to the vernacular. This 1991 brochure puts black-letter back on the menu as Zuzana Licko argued for her Totally Gothic. "It seems curious," she wrote, "that black-letter typestyles, which we find illegible today, were actually preferred over more humanistic designs during the eleventh and fifteenth centuries. Similarly typestyles that we perceive as illegible today may well become tomorrow's classic choices." Above: cover of the magazine *Domus*, September 1991, art directed by Italo Lupi. Notable for its espousal of OCR-A as a headline face – once the manifestation of intermediate computer technology, by 1991 a post-modern reference. **p.147**

landscape for typographic activity and for type design. As suggested previously, it became customary over this decade for type to be designed, "set" and output using computers. In fact, this revolution essentially removed the notion of typesetting, thereby abandoning an area of craft skill along with the repetition of keystrokes. The lack of a trained compositor's eye on type led to a general decay in controls over much commonplace printing.

The radical lowering in the price and increase in the processing-power and functionality of technology changed the cultural meaning of typography, as well as the conditions for production. During the 1990s it became possible for anyone with a few hundred dollars to buy a computer on which type could be designed and typographic material laid

out. For example, the Apple Macintosh series of computers (which despite various business problems maintained a lead in the creative business areas of design and communication) went from being expensive tools to being comparatively inexpensive, targeted as much for home use as heavy business activity.

The first Macintosh (of 1984) cost more than a top-of-the-range model with vastly increased functionality ten years later, with no adjustment for inflation. In 1990, desktop publishing techniques (digital authoring and transfer of materials for publishing) were still being pioneered and were starting to move rapidly beyond the stage of "early adopters" in the leading Western countries. By 1995 it was commonplace and by 1997 it was a fundamental

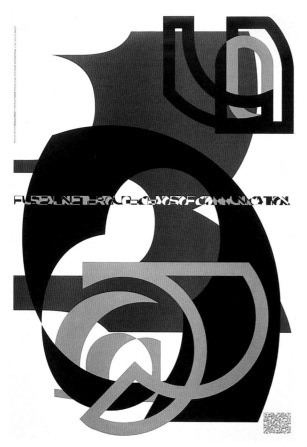

Berliner *24pt*

X-Fuse Fontur *12pt*

All images and faces on these pages are part of the Fuse project started in 1991 by Neville Brody and Jon Wozencroft. This has involved the publication of a small magazine with disk containing experimental fonts and a set of posters by the font designers exploring their font. The new faces were not intended as useful, but questioned type and communication. Brody's State, 1991, seen in the poster shown left, set the tone of the investigation. It sought "to get inside the structure of the alphabet and to accentuate the shapes that are inherent in written language...". While Brody said it was not for day-to-day use, he added: "Readability is a conditioned state. I wanted to take the typography away from a purely subservient, practical role towards one that is potentially more expressive and visually dynamic...." The image shown opposite is by the Swiss designer Cornel Windlin with his font Moon Base Alpha – one that has begun to find its way into more everyday use despite its "unconventional" readability.

Whatthehell *18pt*

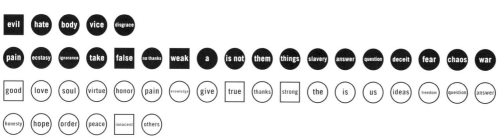

part of the design business practice the world over. While hand-set, hot-metal and photoset practices could all still be seen, sometimes through harsh economic circumstances and sometimes through a more aesthetically-motivated regard for the old craft, the basic mode of production was rapidly switched to the digital source and output of type.

The confusing statistics of the computer revolution are many and varied, depending on the purpose and point of measurement. Projections for internet use alone vary from a predicted global ubiquity to a meltdown of the system. However, a personal anecdote may illustrate: I visited a design college in the Siberian capital Novosibirsk in April

1997. No printed matter on this city was readily available, but more than ten thousand internet sites existed, delivering a selection of sunny photographs and extensive data on the weather and suchlike, albeit thrown down the line with my default font driving out long line-lengths of closely set Times. On arrival at the real (rather than virtual) city, it was clear that road and building maintenance programmes were short of funds. Civic pride was summarized by the lack of any postcards, except for reluctantly-proffered images of 1960s Communist monuments and other showpieces. However, at the college, powerful Macintosh and Sun computers matched the technology available in many Western schools, and within design, advertising and print companies similar technology was commonplace.

**Moon Base** *48pt*

ABCDEFGHIJKL
MNOPQRSTUWXYZ

**Freeform One** *24pt*

**Atomic Circle** *12pt*

**Flixel** *18pt*

**Bits** *18pt*

**Crash** *12pt*

The point of this story is that while large differences in physical, cultural and economic conditions may exist between and within nations, the technology within which typographic activity largely takes place has linked (or is linking) around the world. Using earlier technologies is in many ways not an option. The digital technology is the only one that provides a gateway to the digital media of today – it is simply not possible to stick with an earlier technology and still contribute to most contemporary publishing, or the "new media" of internet and multimedia. This has helped determine a "melting pot" of activity in the creation and delivery of material like never before. The nature of the internet often goes further to iron out differences, producing an illusion of greater similarity.

The material in this book has concentrated on an Anglo-American dominance in technology and much of typographic theory, since it is the imperialist communications culture that has mostly led the evolution of type. The march of that technology and culture has worked with the development of a world where English has become the most international language – but now, just when the triumph of Western political, economic and cultural thought may be at its zenith, it is at its most exposed to new influences.

Consider the potential of the project to develop Unicode, a character-encoding standard, designed to enable a global interchange of multilingual information. The leading hardware and software companies have supported this and an International Standard has been written around it. It envisages a set of up to sixty-five thousand characters, drawing together the many different scripts and symbols that are used typographically around the world. Unicode-compliant software and hardware is expected to enable keyboards to readily configure to the appropriate characters via a selection menu. The only problem, as Robin Nicholas, head of typography at Monotype Typography observed in 1997, was the task of designing coherent fonts that carried the necessary characters. In practice you might assemble "font sets" that covered the options, but still, there is the emerging need for global sign systems that have coherence and can carry consistent messages, such as brand identities. Multinational corporations are beginning to manage their identity programmes by making the information available on intranets, centrally holding typographic and other data,

ensuring its accurate transcription to all parts of the world. Rather like "world music", which has fed into individual music cultures around the world, it is possible that global typographic information is coming together to influence its various parts in ways inconceivable without the current creative and media technologies.

While the thought of a sixty-five thousand character set might suggest a lifetime's work for a (still young) type designer, the changed experience of type design in this period was that a new font might actually be knocked up in a day, since it became possible, using desktop font design software, to draw or modify letterforms very quickly. Of course, instant letterforms were unlikely to result in a lasting, usable typeface, but no longer were the means of

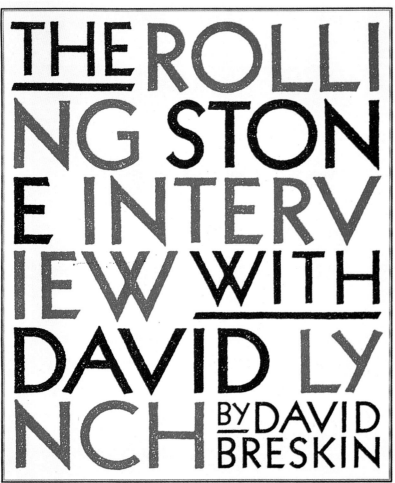

58 · ROLLING STONE, SEPTEMBER 6TH, 1990

Expressive typography has spread across editorial and advertising worldwide in the 1990s, partly as a result of the ease and economics of the publishing technology now compared with pre-digital days. However, certain art directors are major influences – Fabien Baron's work on Italian *Vogue*, then *Interview*, shown opposite from April 1990, and subsequently *Harper's Bazaar* in the US, has pioneered typo-illustration as a powerful and elegant tool within fashion and style publications. And the strong typographic feature openers of *Rolling Stone*, as practised since 1987 by the art director Fred Woodward, have celebrated calligraphy, wood letter, and more contemporary type, as highly expressive editorial tools. Shown left is one page of an opener spread from 1990, that faced a portrait of the subject, David Lynch.

production and testing the factor in determining the time of type creation.

The internet, of course, is seen as a central manifestation of that, but its typographic controls were initially primitive. The instruction code for laying out pages (Hypertext Mark-up Language [HTML]) provided only rudimentary controls – such as setting left, centring or set right and the user's default font is either much to the fore, or else larger image files have to be incorporated in the page where words are depicted as images, thus slowing down the delivery of the information. OpenType, mentioned above, might be the solution.

Looking back over the century, from near the end of the final decade in a millennium, we have an acute sensitivity to the benefit of hindsight. There is a temptation to make conclusions – to see ourselves at the end of something, or at the cutting edge, or at the burnt-out conclusion. Our raised position provokes the thought that today designers work within a typographic context that could scarcely have been dreamt of by a previous generation – or, indeed, this generation a decade or so earlier, so fast has been the change. And yet our current excitement over all things digital can also be read as the fulfilment of half-progressed experiments and the principles behind earlier movements. Imagine what the Bauhaus would have done with the internet! And wasn't Cubism just anticipating the four-dimensional explorations of multimedia? This is, of course, to post-rationalize the past with the concerns and characteristics of today. To read the data assembled from our

David Carson became the most widely celebrated graphic designer of the 1990s, thanks to his typographic pyrotechnics on the magazines *Beach Culture* (1990-1), right, and *Ray Gun* (1993-5), opposite top, and the subsequent bestselling books (both created with the current author) *The End of Print* and *2ndsight*, opposite bottom. His highly expressive use of type, which at times would be used more like paint or collage elements than for its linear reading sense, has won him many critics as well as fanatical support. His approach has been at the centre of a movement of younger designers towards making expressive, personally indulgent work, at the expense of any designer anonymity. His "Zapf Dingbat" spread, opposite, shows a whole magazine feature set in an unreadable font of symbols – Carson's personal reaction to the dull text. The *2ndsight* spread shows his move away from an early concentration on editorial and into work for advertising and, here, a website for MGM.

bryan rally

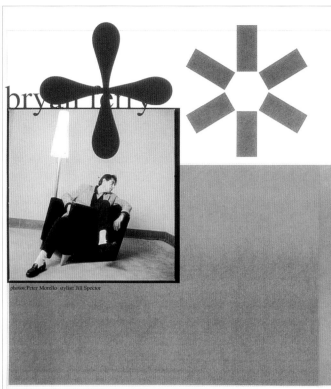

photos: Peter Morello  stylist: Jill Spector

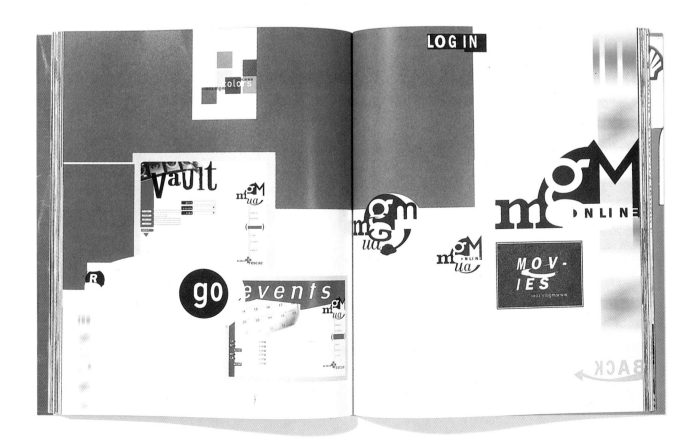

excavation of typographic history only in the terms that come easily to mind now, obscures the complexity of matters past, as well as present. To do so is the opposite of the true aim of historical enquiry, and yet every historian ends up at such a point if they are ever to publish. This book, inevitably, does more than a little of that, being both short, heavily illustrated (by a fraction of the production it purports to cover) and deliberately weighted to noting the avant-garde rather than the living traditions of design. It is a primer to prompt research, a tool for probing notions of the past and present, and a basic scrapbook for experimentation in the practice of graphic design.

Since we can only interpret in the light of what we now know, whether it is the basic recognition of character forms or of the meaning of words, or the ability to see visual and verbal connections and proceed to some kind of analysis, we are condemned to remix the past to make the present. The flexibility of digital design and its output in print or on screen has created possibilities, but this is a new world made from the scrapings of the old, and displays many familiar obsessions. Consider how the internet browser interface design as used by Netscape Navigator and Microsoft Explorer (the two overwhelmingly dominant products of the mid-1990s "browser war") follow the graphical-user-interface (GUI) model pioneered by the Apple Macintosh and then largely copied by Microsoft Windows software. This is the basic computing environment experienced by content authors and users in the desktop publishing world. And this in itself was taken from technology pioneered at Xerox in the

Left and above: since its inception in 1991, FontShop International has been to the fore in building strong distribution alliances and promoting its new releases with wit and commercial relevance – as seen here with font sampler being shown applied to vernacular signage. Left is a range of weights developing the German standard DIN by Albert-Jan Pool, 1995, and Info, 1996, by Erik Spiekermann and Ole Schäfer, while above is an ingenious re-working of OCR by Pool in 1995 to provide it in differing weights. Opposite: Mark Farrow has been a prime exponent of minimalist typography in the 1990s, an increasingly credible route against the endless type design and typographic diversity brought about by the digital explosion. This poster was for the Hacienda club in Manchester, England, and gained its impact from being printed in fluorescent ink so that the type stood out at night.

late 1970s, and derived in turn from computing science thinkers in the 1960s (we have still only crudely realized the promise of Ted Nelson's 1965 dream of non-linear "hypertext"). The virtual desktop of flat icons that dominates the appearance of software tools is a graphic display derived from the print culture people are familiar with, rather than truly embracing the fluid forms possible on screen.

This conservatism in form is the comfortable path, and is to a certain extent inevitable. The tendency towards appropriating or emulating traditional forms in new media goes back to the first printed book, when Gutenberg drew on manuscript precedents for his bible of 1452. Handwriting has continued to have some link to type form. Now, on-screen type draws on print media. From 1997, the leaders of digital and web typography, Adobe and Microsoft, actively encouraged a narrow orthodoxy for web typography by promoting a special restricted palette of twelve or so web-friendly fonts on their internet sites. This was presented as a way of improving web typography, in that if web developers coded sites to work with these fonts, which were commonly available on users' systems, then crude type defaults would be less necessary. Nevertheless, the imposition of a new orthodoxy is involved. And while Adobe's Myriad and Minion already had a popular following, this could not be said for other faces proffered in the launch series. The free distribution might also alarm those companies who depend on font sales for their livelihood (unlike Adobe and Microsoft).

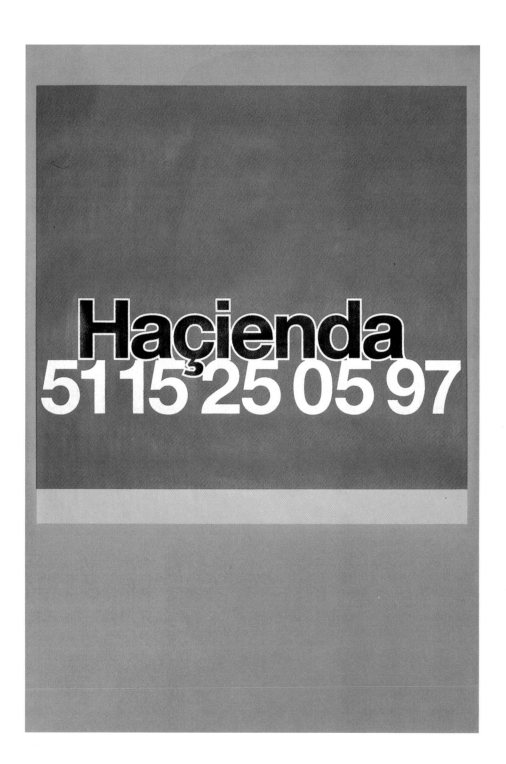

Such thinking at best seems concerned with evolution, rather than revolution. It is in the advances made in the "typographic engine" and in probing three-dimensional, even four-dimensional typographic forms, that we see paths opening towards a strange new landscape of typographic form. Typefaces which fit comfortably on the page of printed type catalogues would not seem to be the future – we already have an awful lot of those. But understanding how type can work on screen, and having the full range of faces to use in both virtual three-dimensional graphic movements, and in the fourth dimension of time-based change are major challenges for type designers and typographers to embrace. Crucially, programmers and the software company patrons need to be working alongside the type designers.

The early experiments of three-dimensional and time-based modulating type forms, and those typographies which probe the organizational issues of virtual four-dimensional space, are perhaps the most pertinent attempts to address the radical agenda of our age. So-called "intelligent" fonts (whose form responds to the user in such a way that it modulates, randomly changes between options, or destabilizes) were pioneered by Just van Rossum and Erik van Blokland with Beowolf in 1990 and have grown to become a new type classification. The remarkable three-dimensional experimental elaborations led by J. Abbott Miller in the Dimensional Typography project of 1996 also suggest the potential of the very different environment in which type and typography now exist on screen. The various experimental, often unreadable symbol-based fonts developed by the Fuse project (see pages 148–9) also explore the dynamic of the typographic engine in a way that steps beyond the expectations and strictures of our conventional alphabets.

It is this concept of type as involving a computerized organism for generating text that may be the most significant typographic development to emerge from the 1990s. Type is not a description of something that is always precise, a character or a font. In the 1990s, type has changed from being something physical (metal, film) to being just information. The type exists only as instructions for bitmaps or bezier curves that construct the letter through mathematics. These maths can involve random elements as well as fixed data. What we commonly call type – the

characters on the screen or on the page – are in some ways only an illusion pushed out to a particular resolution by an imagesetter or laserwriter.

The potential of screen-based communication suggests that intelligent fonts active across virtual space and time – anticipating, aiding and stimulating the reader/viewer – could be a basic tool for multimedia and internet content creation and use. Type is just starting to act and to move beyond its life as the printed word.

**These new typefaces are called "Multiple Masters"** because two or more sets of outlines, or *master designs*, are integrated into each typeface. The master designs determine the *dynamic range* of each design axis in a typeface, and the PostScript® language enables on-demand interpolation, or generation of intermediate variations, between the master designs. For example, a light and a black master design delineate the dynamic range of possible font variations along the weight design axis, and the user can interpolate variations anywhere within this range. The particular design axes which comprise each Multiple Master typeface are based on the aesthetics and potential uses of that typeface; therefore, the number of design axes and their ranges vary from one Multiple Master typeface to another. Some of the possible design axes include weight, width, style, and optical size, which are briefly described below.

design axis ▼

dynamic range

With Multiple Master typefaces, the concept of a typeface family is essentially redefined. A typical contemporary typeface family contains only three or four different weights. Multiple Master typefaces with a *weight axis* make it possible for users to generate additional weight variations to customize the typeface family to specific needs.

weight

aaaaaaaaaaaaaa

*light to black*

Only a few typeface families supply either condensed or expanded versions of the basic design, consequently the practice of artificially compressing or stretching existing typefaces is widespread. Multiple Master typefaces with a *width axis* allow the creation of fonts of varying widths without any distortion of the letterforms.

width

aaaaaaaaaaaa

*condensed to extended*

The potential for typographic expression with Multiple Master typefaces with a *style axis* is nearly limitless. For example, Multiple Master typefaces with a style axis could incorporate design variations that range from sans serif to serif, inline to decorated, or wedge serif to slab serif, to name just a few possibilities.

style

aaaaaaaaaaaaa

*wedge serif to slab serif*

In traditional metal typefounding each style and point size of a typeface was cut by hand, incorporating subtle adjustments to letter proportion, weight, contrast, and spacing so that the type would be optimized for readability in every point size. Multiple Master typefaces with an *optical size axis* reintroduce the practice of optically adjusting type, allowing users to generate highly readable fonts over a full range of point sizes.

optical size

aaaaaaaaaaaa

*6 point to 72 point (scaled to same size)*

The long quest for a universal typeface did not disappear in the 1990s, but the precise objectives varied. Erik Spiekermann's Meta, 1993, opposite left, addressed the need for a highly durable and adaptable text font for wide use across differing print and screen environments. It offers extensive variations. Lucas de Groot's Thesis, 1989-94, opposite right, has three dramatic variations – TheSans, TheSerif and TheMix. Each of these is in eight weights. Each weight is in six variants (plain, italic, small caps, small caps italic, expert and expert italic). This made a total of 144 fonts and more than 32,000 characters in the initial release of the font. Meanwhile, Adobe's multiple masters technology has sought to put type choice into an intelligent engine, whereby users can manipulate a font to a suitable design through altering the nature of a font along sliding axes, such as on weight or width. Myriad (promotional book shown left) and Minion, launched in 1991, were the first faces to sport the new technology, which has been slow in being adopted. **p.157**

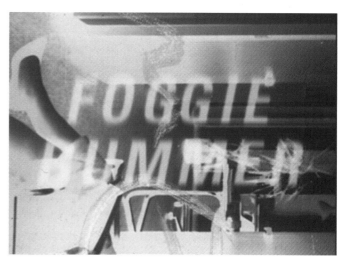

Above: stills from Foggie Bummer, 1995, for BBC Radio Scotland, designed by Jon Barnbrook. Animated typography on screen has proliferated in television titles and commercials, and this spot was one of six (three directed by Barnbrook, three by tomato) that were internationally recognized. The campaign asked the designers to animate the spoken word, concentrating on the power of the language. Left: an early font by Barnbrook, who now has his own "foundry", Virus.

**Bastard-Even Fatter** *36pt*

ABCDEFGHIJKLM
NOPQRSTUVWXYZ
abcdefghijklmnopqrstuvwxyz

The diversity of 1990s design was matched by type makers – with Emigre as likely to publish a font of ornamental devices driven out of the typographic engine, such as Hypnopaedia by Zuzana Licko, 1997, launch promotion above, as add to its explorations of late Modernism. Right: The Hoefler Type Foundry catalogue typifies how individual type designers moved into self-publishing and distribution, a late 1990s phenomenon that, thanks to the internet, could become the standard distribution method.

Right: stills from an interactive multimedia project by antirom with tomato and underworld, built around a font by Don Nendle, 1997, published by Creative Review, London. Type forms were attached to sound loops and three-dimensional movement, enabling the user to compose sound/image pieces with the software. Work such as this proposes an opportunity for type to move beyond the terms of its print or televisual life. Below right: Jesus Loves You by Lucas de Groot, 1995, one of the new genre of fonts described by its distributor FSI as "destructives" for their deconstructive take on letterforms. This font was one of those taken in the Dimensional Typography project, 1995/6, example characters opposite, led by J. Abbott Miller of New York studio Design/Writing/Research. Jesus Loves You became Rhizome (the resulting lower case "j" is shown opposite top, viewed from above). The other character is from Polymorphous, a 3D development of Zuzana Licko's 1995 font Modula Ribbed. The line drawing is from the wire frame used to build such forms. "The ability to think of letterforms as having spatial and temporal dimension brings with it new obligations and opportunities to augment the visual and editorial power of letters," says Miller, who points out that the methods of visual development, such as extrusion, rotation, shadowing and more, are not new to the era of virtual environments, but lie behind the history of type design.

type production has gone mad, with its senseless outpouring of new types... only in degenerate times can personality (opposed to the nameless masses) become the aim of human development. See introduction for credit.

Left: character from the revived Mongolian script, adopted as the national writing standard for Mongolia in 1994 following the abolition of the Soviet-imposed Cyrillic alphabet. Part of a 270-character set drawn in 1992 in order to produce new children's elementary textbooks.

**Analysis of characters**

**Apex** The outside point at which two strokes meet, as at the top of an *A* or *M*, or at the bottom of *M*.

**Arm** The projecting horizontal or upward stroke not enclosed within a character, as in *E*, *K* or *L*.

**Ascender** The lower-case letter *stem* that rises above the *x-height*, as in *b*, *d* or *k*.

**Baseline** The line on which the *x-height* rests.

**Body clearance** The space between the character and the edge of the unit.

**Body size** The unit height on which the character is mounted. See also *Point size*.

**Bowl** The oval stroke that encloses the *counter*, as in *b*, *p* or *O*.

**Bracket** A curving joint between the *serif* and the *stem*.

**Cap height** The height of the upper case in a font, taken from the *baseline* to the top of the character.

**Cicero** European unit of typographical measurement, equal to 12 *corps*. This is slightly smaller than the UK and US equivalent of one *pica* or 12 points, at 4.155mm.

**Corps** European measurement of *point* or *body size*, but slightly smaller than the UK and US equivalents.

**Counter** The white space within a *bowl*.

**Crossbar** The horizontal stroke in *A*, *H*, *f* or *t*; also known as a bar or a cross-stroke.

**Descender** The lower-case letter *stem* or lower part that falls below the *baseline*, as in *p* or *g*.

**Ear** A small projecting stroke sometimes attached to the *bowl* of the *g* or the *stem* of the *r*.

**Leg** The downwards oblique stroke of the *R* and *K*; can also be called the *tail*.

**Link** A connecting stroke when the *g* has a *bowl* and *loop*.

**Loop** The portion of the *g* that falls below the *baseline* when it is entirely closed.
**Pica** Unit of typographical measurement equal to 12 *points*, 1/6 or 0.166 of an inch or 4.218mm.
**Point** The basic unit of typographical measurement, approximately 1/72 or 0.0138 of an inch or 0.351mm.
**Point size** Equivalent to the body size, the height of body on which the type is cast (even if, with today's technology, it is rarely "cast").
**Serif** The small stroke drawn across and out of a *stem*, *arm* or *tail*.
**Spine** The main curved stroke of an *S* or *s*.
**Spur** The projection seen sometimes on the bottom of a *b* or *G*.
**Stem** The principal vertical or oblique stroke in a letter, as in *L*, *B*, *V* or *A*.
**Stress** The inclination suggested by the relationship of thick and thin strokes in a letter. Characters can have an inclined or a vertical stress.
**Stroke** The principal line within a character.
**Tail** The short stroke that rests on the *baseline* in *R* and *K*, or below it in *Q*.

In *R* and *K* it can also be called the *leg*.
**x-height** The lower-case character height when *ascenders* and *descenders* are excluded.

bowl    stem    ascender    arm    vertical stress    counter    inclined stress

body clearance

spur    bowl    leg    tail    bowl

**p.165**

# Type description and classification

Describing and classifying type has exercised many sharp minds, provoked many an argument, and led to continuing debate. The explosion in the variety of type design, and shift in its method of production and its purpose, has hugely exacerbated the problem of giving order to the world of type. So why bother? There are two principal reasons: one is practical, in that description and classification helps to make it possible to trace a typeface; the second is that this process of analysis enables us to see patterns within the forms, and possibly discern some directions, some meaning, behind the invention of new forms.

Various methods of analysis are used to identify the attributes of individual type characters, the fonts to which they belong, the families of fonts, and the contrasting and comparative groupings that can be made between them. While these methods try to explain matters, they can also be confusing. This is because differing terms, tables and systems of measurement have been devised over centuries of typographic evolution. As new ideas and new technologies have changed the nature of type, so new forms of typographic practice have emerged to challenge the classification systems. With a subject such as measurement, the issue is by its nature fairly precisely defined and different systems can be readily compared. The description of character attributes – stem, serif, bowl and so on – is also comparatively straightforward, although there are points at which verbal definitions of visual forms run into problems (for example, where does a serif simply become the flared termination of a stroke?).

The larger descriptive problem arises when typefaces are assigned to different categories. Typeface categories have emerged by evolution, one form developing from another and a range of faces being produced as a result, but their relationship is not explained by describing them only along historical lines. The revised categories devised by the typographic historian Maximilien Vox in the 1950s, which were widely adopted in various guises, now prove inadequate for explaining the huge number of new typeface designs since. A digital black-letter face, for instance, such as can be seen in the 1990s, has several reference points, while some modern re-drawings of earlier faces make changes (such as increasing the x-height) that effectively

convert them into a different face from the one the name would suggest. Even the apparently simple split between serif and sans serif is complicated by designs with "flared serifs" such as Optima, or a face such as Copperplate Gothic, in which the minuscule terminus strokes are intended to assert the squared ends of the stroke rather than act as clear serifs. Adobe's multiple master fonts push out designs that can be altered by the user and range across classifications, while Beowolf began a culture of fonts that had an "organic" element within them of shifting design within set parameters. Classifiers have been challenged to find new methods of describing typefaces, and have yet to propose anything at all universally accepted. Different font distributors use different systems, and weaknesses can be easily picked in them. Some have no categories, some have titles that seem more led by their marketing considerations than by any rational structure. Meanwhile, research projects probe and suggest new descriptors. Our system draws on the Vox classification of historical groups, while adding subdivisions and extensions to cover less conventional forms and contemporary design. The categories are guidelines... redefine, remix the systems if you can.

All faces are presented here in 18 point, output from twentieth-century designs that have been digitized. They are indications of the faces, rather than definitive cuts – different technologies, different printing surfaces or output media, make different impressions. For a true idea of, say, the work of Manutius or Garamond, nothing matches seeing an original. In the original context it is possible to see why certain letterforms were designed – to cope with inkspread, to work in certain sizes and resolutions. These classifications cover the principal areas of typeface design discussed in the book, so do not include non-Latin typefaces or symbols. I suspect a further remix of the book will bring in new classifications, or indeed see a replacement of the essentially historical basis for this model by an altogether more synchronic analysis of content.

# Humanist

# Abefgor

Kennerley

## Horley Old Style

abcdefghijklmnopqrstuvwxyz
ABCDEFGHIJKLMNOPQRSTUVWXYZ
1234567890

## Jenson-Eusebius

abcdefghijklmnopqrstuvwxyz
ABCDEFGHIJKLMNOPQRSTUVWXYZ
1234567890

## Cloister

abcdefghijklmnopqrstuvwxyz
ABCDEFGHIJKLMNOPQRSTUVWXYZ
1234567890

## Kennerley

abcdefghijklmnopqrstuvwxyz
ABCDEFGHIJKLMNOPQRSTUVWXYZ
1234567890

A group of faces that take their inspiration from the early roman style, in particular the work of Nicolas Jenson (1420–80), a French printer whose most notable work was produced in the last decade of his life during which he lived in Venice. The face is based upon humanist writing seen in fifteenth-century manuscripts, as opposed to the black-letter hand that Gutenberg used for the first printing with movable type in the 1450s. Humanist writing was rounder and broader, and was produced with a broad-nibbed pen that helped give certain inflections. (The angle of stress in these faces matches the diagonal stress that would be given to, say, an "O" if it were drawn with a broad-nibbed pen held at an angle to the page.) The features that distinguish humanist faces from later romans are: a sloping bar on the "e", a marked inclination of stress backwards to the left, and little contrast between thick and thin strokes. Several foundries produced revivals of the face seen in Jenson's books. Cloister Old Style, by Morris Fuller Benton for American Type Founders in 1897, was the first revival of the mechanical composition era; William Morris's Golden drew on Jenson's face, as did Doves, but these were more loosely derived. Frederic Goudy's Kennerley of 1911 and Bruce Rogers' Centaur of 1914/1929 are based on Jenson, while having several differences: for example, Kennerley has noticeably shorter descenders and Centaur is generally lighter. The distinctive sloping bar characteristic of the group is displayed in Horley Old Style, a compact and robust face produced by Monotype in 1925, which in other respects is closer to a later garalde roman.

# Abefgor Sabon

## Sabon

abcdefghijklmnopqrstuvwxyz
ABCDEFGHIJKLMNOPQRSTUVWXYZ
1234567890

## Garamond

abcdefghijklmnopqrstuvwxyz
ABCDEFGHIJKLMNOPQRSTUVWXYZ
1234567890

## Bembo

abcdefghijklmnopqrstuvwxyz
ABCDEFGHIJKLMNOPQRSTUVWXYZ
1234567890

## Times New Roman

abcdefghijklmnopqrstuvwxyz
ABCDEFGHIJKLMNOPQRSTUVWXYZ
1234567890

These faces, formerly called Old Face or Old Style, have a horizontal bar to the "e" but in other respects share features with the humanist grouping. Pen-influenced characteristics such as the oblique stroke on lower-case ascender serifs are still present and the characters tend to have a backwards slope (although not always as pronounced as in humanist). Contrasts between thick and thin strokes are more marked. The first models for garalde faces are those of the Venetian printer Aldus Manutius (1450–1515) and the punchcutter he worked with, Francesco Griffo. These faces were used in the Aldine Press books from the late 1490s onwards. The twentieth-century revival form Bembo (Monotype, 1929, and later other founders) takes its name from Cardinal Bembo's *De Aetna* of 1495, the book in which the Manutius/Griffo face was first noted. It was the sixteenth-century French typecutter and designer Claude Garamond (1500–61) who was the first to produce a notable reworking of the Aldine Press faces, creating a face seen from the 1530s onwards that has been redrawn by most foundries in the twentieth century for their own Garamonds. Granjon, based on the face associated with the sixteenth-century French type designer Robert Granjon, is close to Garamond, and the characteristics are still there in the eighteenth-century Caslon, itself modelled on seventeenth-century Dutch designs, such as those associated with Christophe Plantin. Stanley Morison's Times New Roman of 1932, while having short ascenders and descenders typical of newspaper type, in other respects takes its idea of stress and contrast from a Plantin-Caslon tradition.

## Plantin

abcdefghijklmnopqrstuvwxyz
ABCDEFGHIJKLMNOPQRSTUVWXYZ
1234567890

## Palatino

abcdefghijklmnopqrstuvwxyz
ABCDEFGHIJKLMNOPQRSTUVWXYZ
1234567890

## Caslon Old Face

abcdefghijklmnopqrstuvwxyz
ABCDEFGHIJKLMNOPQRSTUVWXYZ
1234567890

Hermann Zapf's Palatino of 1950, named after a sixteenth-century Italian calligrapher, drew on Italian Renaissance lettering along with Roman inscriptions, which helps explain its generous counters and unorthodox serifs on the outside only of certain letters. Jan Tschichold's Sabon is a garalde that was designed to work across the various composition technologies (hand, hot metal and photocomposition when he drew it in the 1960s).

# Abefgor

## Baskerville

abcdefghijklmnopqrstuvwxyz
ABCDEFGHIJKLMNOPQRSTUVWXYZ
1234567890

## Caslon

abcdefghijklmnopqrstuvwxyz
ABCDEFGHIJKLMNOPQRSTUVWXYZ
1234567890

## Fournier

abcdefghijklmnopqrstuvwxyz
ABCDEFGHIJKLMNOPQRSTUVWXYZ
1234567890

## Perpetua

abcdefghijklmnopqrstuvwxyz
ABCDEFGHIJKLMNOPQRSTUVWXYZ
1234567890

Transitional faces are so called because they have characters that show the transition from the "old style" garalde to the "modern" didone faces that first emerged in the late eighteenth century. Transitional typefaces tend to be more upright than garaldes, with either a vertical or only slightly inclined stress. They may also have more contrast. Serifs may be bracketed and oblique as before, or horizontal and tending towards the starkness of the didone serif. The faces of the English typographer John Baskerville (1706–75) and the French founder Pierre Fournier (1712–68) are central to this grouping, while its links with what came before are suggested by the inclusion in the category of some twentieth-century reworkings of Caslon and Garamond. W.A. Dwiggins' Caledonia of 1938 is a transitional that incorporates aspects of the didone style: horizontal serifs are lightly bracketed and shade into an unbracketed "t".

# Didone

# Abefgor

## Bauer Bodoni

abcdefghijklmnopqrstuvwxyz
ABCDEFGHIJKLMNOPQRSTUVWXYZ
1234567890

## Bodoni

abcdefghijklmnopqrstuvwxyz
ABCDEFGHIJKLMNOPQRSTUVWXYZ
1234567890

## Torino

abcdefghijklmnopqrstuvwxyz
ABCDEFGHIJKLMNOPQRSTUVWXYZ
1234567890

## Walbaum

abcdefghijklmnopqrstuvwxyz
ABCDEFGHIJKLMNOPQRSTUVWXYZ
1234567890

Here the contrast between thick and thin strokes is extreme; lower-case serifs are horizontal and often unbracketed; the stress is vertical. These characteristics were exemplified in the work of Giambattista Bodoni (1740–1813) of Parma, who took the French types of Fournier and the Didots and refined them to the characteristics outlined above. Firmin Didot had produced the first didone – hence the name for the group – in Paris in the 1780s (the printing company bearing the name still exists on the Left Bank). Didot's thin serifs and abrupt contrasts involved hairline strokes that took advantage of improved paper and printing to create a more elegant typography. Bodoni's cuts made the most of this approach to typeface design, and his layouts displayed a generous use of white space that drew out the sparkling, high-contrast qualities of the face. Several twentieth-century revivals of his face attempt to retain these qualities while making it more efficient in its demands on space (for example, while the ATF cutting was the first and most commonly followed, the Bauer Bodoni is a more refined but less robust version). Torino is an early twentieth-century revival from the Nebiolo foundry with exaggerated serifs and other terminal flourishes, while Didi ITC is an exaggerated form of didone created for display purposes by Bonder and Carnase in 1970. Walbaum, a wider and less rounded didone, is based on designs by the German punchcutter Justus Erich Walbaum (1768–1839), who favoured the Didot style rather than that of Bodoni.

# Abefgor

Bookman

---

## Bookman

abcdefghijklmnopqrstuvwxyz
ABCDEFGHIJKLMNOPQRSTUVWXYZ
1234567890

---

## Century Schoolbook

abcdefghijklmnopqrstuvwxyz
ABCDEFGHIJKLMNOPQRSTUVWXYZ
1234567890

---

## Cheltenham

abcdefghijklmnopqrstuvwxyz
ABCDEFGHIJKLMNOPQRSTUVWXYZ
1234567890

This group covers those serif faces that display a complex, hybrid mix of features that do not feature in the previous historical evolution of form. They are sturdier faces than the thin didones, often originally cut in the nineteenth century to overcome problems of reproduction as larger print runs, poorer-quality papers and the demand for more compact faces put the typefaces of finer printing under stresses they were not capable of meeting. Bookman was originally a mid-nineteenth-century face, revived again in the 1920s; originally called Antique Old Style, it boasted a composite of features rather than being a straightforward garalde. Century Schoolbook, designed by Morris Fuller Benton and released in 1915, was – as the name suggests – intended for schoolbooks and is based on Century, the slightly condensed face designed by Linn Boyd Benton in the 1890s for the *Century* magazine. Upright stress, short ascenders and descenders and heavy serifs are all elements that make for its compact but legible letters. Excelsior, a newspaper face of 1931, has similar features since it strives for maximum legibility under stressful printing conditions. The massive popularity of the Cheltenham family, originally begun in the 1890s, was based upon its robustness and maintenance of character across many weights, widths, sizes and other variations.

# Slab-serif

# Abefgor

Memphis

## Clarendon

abcdefghijklmnopqrstuvwxyz
ABCDEFGHIJKLMNOPQRSTUVWXYZ
1234567890

## Memphis

abcdefghijklmnopqrstuvwxyz
ABCDEFGHIJKLMNOPQRSTUVWXYZ
1234567890

## Serifa

abcdefghijklmnopqrstuvwxyz
ABCDEFGHIJKLMNOPQRSTUVWXYZ
1234567890

## Calvert

abcdefghijklmnopqrstuvwxyz
ABCDEFGHIJKLMNOPQRSTUVWXYZ
1234567890

The name says it: those typefaces with heavy, square-ended serifs, with or without brackets. Clarendon, released by R. Besley & Co. in 1845, was the prototype slab-serif – indeed, "Clarendon" was used as a general descriptive for similar faces. Its clarity and sturdiness made it suitable for emphasis in text setting as well as for widespread use in display forms, such as posters. Robert Harling's Playbill of 1938 was an extreme form that made the serifs heavier than the main strokes in an imitation of Victorian playbill style. The late 1920s and early 1930s saw a major revival of slab-serif forms, with Memphis by Rudolf Weiss (1929) leading the way and proving the most lasting, along with Monotype's Rockwell. Serifa, by Adrian Frutiger and launched in 1967, is a slab-serif version of his earlier sans serif Univers. Calvert, by Margaret Calvert and released by Monotype in 1980, was based on signage lettering she designed for the Tyne and Wear Metro.

# Abefgor

News Gothic

**Franklin Gothic**

abcdefghijklmnopqrstuvwxyz
ABCDEFGHIJKLMNOPQRSTUVWXYZ
1234567890

**News Gothic**

abcdefghijklmnopqrstuvwxyz
ABCDEFGHIJKLMNOPQRSTUVWXYZ
1234567890

**Trade Gothic**

abcdefghijklmnopqrstuvwxyz
ABCDEFGHIJKLMNOPQRSTUVWXYZ
1234567890

The first lineales, or sans serifs, can be found in catalogues at the beginning of the nineteenth century; they were bulky and tended to exist only in the upper case. Wood-letter forms existed, but were restricted to large-scale display use. At the beginning of the twentieth century there was interest in the form with the growth of display print needs, and Morris Fuller Benton was quick to cover the market for ATF with Alternate Gothic (1903), Franklin Gothic (1904) and News Gothic (1908). The strokes have contrast and there is a squared-off crudeness to the curves. The later Trade Gothic, by Jackson Burke (1948), is altogether smoother; however, Franklin Gothic has more than stood the test of time to remain immensely popular in editorial and advertising.

Lineale b. Neo-grotesque

# Abefgor

Univers

## Akzidenz Grotesk

abcdefghijklmnopqrstuvwxyz
ABCDEFGHIJKLMNOPQRSTUVWXYZ
1234567890

## Folio

abcdefghijklmnopqrstuvwxyz
ABCDEFGHIJKLMNOPQRSTUVWXYZ
1234567890

## Helvetica

abcdefghijklmnopqrstuvwxyz
ABCDEFGHIJKLMNOPQRSTUVWXYZ
1234567890

## Univers

abcdefghijklmnopqrstuvwxyz
ABCDEFGHIJKLMNOPQRSTUVWXYZ
1234567890

These are similar to the grotesque grouping of lineales, but the stroke width contrasts are less marked. This means that the characters show more signs of being designed than of retaining any pen-drawn characteristics. The jaws of letters such as "C" tend to be more open than with the grotesques. The most marked distinction between the two groups is that the neo-grotesques do not have a lower bowl to the "g", but an open stroke. Akzidenz Grotesk, released by Berthold in 1896 and also known as Standard, became popular with the Swiss Style typographers; in the 1950s it underlay the design of Neue Haas Grotesk/Helvetica by Max Miedinger and Edouard Hoffman and also of Univers by Adrian Frutiger. Folio, by Konrad Bauer and Walter Baum of 1957, follows the same pattern. Venus, a Wagner & Schmidt design for Bauer of 1907, had some popularity with the Modern Movement and exists in a wide range of variations.

# Abefgor

## Futura

abcdefghijklmnopqrstuvwxyz
ABCDEFGHIJKLMNOPQRSTUVWXYZ
1234567890

## Kabel

abcdefghijklmnopqrstuvwxyz
ABCDEFGHIJKLMNOPQRSTUVWXYZ
1234567890

## Eurostile

abcdefghijklmnopqrstuvwxyz
ABCDEFGHIJKLMNOPQRSTUVWXYZ
1234567890

## Avant Garde

abcdefghijklmnopqrstuvwxyz
ABCDEFGHIJKLMNOPQRSTUVWXYZ
1234567890

Sans serif faces that follow the rule of being constructed from geometric shapes make up this group. Stroke widths tend to the constant. Chief among them is Futura of 1927, by Paul Renner, a face that quickly grew and kept popularity as it expressed both Modernist ideas and a sense of classic proportions within and between letters. It was widely copied. Erbar (1922), by Jakob Erbar, slightly predates Futura and is similar. Kabel (1927), by Rudolf Koch, is a more individual design that departs at times from the minimalism of its contemporary geometrics. Eurostile (1962) by Aldo Novarese, is sometimes grouped with neo-grotesques, but is essentially geometric in its interpretation of letterforms in relation to the square. Avant Garde Gothic, by Herb Lubalin and Tom Carnase of 1970, developed the geometric model for a face that would have a high degree of legibility in different uses, the numerous upper-case ligatures giving the opportunity for a distinctive character in display applications.

# Abefgor

---

## Gill Sans

abcdefghijklmnopqrstuvwxyz
ABCDEFGHIJKLMNOPQRSTUVWXYZ
1234567890

---

## Optima

abcdefghijklmnopqrstuvwxyz
ABCDEFGHIJKLMNOPQRSTUVWXYZ
1234567890

---

## Goudy Sans

abcdefghijklmnopqrstuvwxyz
ABCDEFGHIJKLMNOPQRSTUVWXYZ
1234567890

---

## Rotis Sans Serif

abcdefghijklmnopqrstuvwxyz
ABCDEFGHIJKLMNOPQRSTUVWXYZ
1234567890

These faces do not so much follow nineteenth-century sans serif precedents as go right back to Roman inscriptions for their roots as well as drawing inspiration from the lower-case hand of humanist writing, which is apparent also in the seriffed humanist and garalde faces. They have some contrast of stroke width. Gill Sans of 1928, by Eric Gill, drew on Edward Johnston's type for the London Underground as well as Gill's signwriting and stone carving that brought him intuitively close to the inscriptional base of the roman forms. Optima, by Hermann Zapf (1958), and Pascal by José Mendoza y Almeida (1960) have notable variations in stroke width that break with the more monotonous line of the geometric and neo-grotesques that were prevailing at the time. Goudy Sans, by Frederic Goudy (1925), is something of a sport, offering variant letterforms and with a pronounced tendency to the inscriptional in the "chiselled" junctions, placing it closer to the glyphic group of faces. The problem of definition is further complicated when considering Rotis, designed by Otl Aicher and released in 1989. The wide range of fonts in the family sit together with design similarities while alluding to different historical roots, the Sans Serif drawing on the humanist lineale tradition.

# Abefgor

---

## Albertus

abcdefghijklmnopqrstuvwxyz
ABCDEFGHIJKLMNOPQRSTUVWXYZ
1234567890

---

## Friz Quadrata

abcdefghijklmnopqrstuvwxyz
ABCDEFGHIJKLMNOPQRSTUVWXYZ
1234567890

---

## Trajan

ABCDEFGHIJKLMNOPQRSTUVWXYZ
1234567890

---

## Amerigo

abcdefghijklmnopqrstuvwxyz
ABCDEFGHIJKLMNOPQRSTUVWXYZ
1234567890

Instead of the calligraphic base, these faces suggest more that they are chiselled than written. They refer back to inscriptional texts rather than the effect of the pen on paper, often taking their inspiration from Roman stonework. The characters tend to be comparatively uniform in width, as if measured out on the page – or stone – before being inscribed. Sharply cut, large, triangular serifs are often used. Albertus, by Berthold Wolpe for Monotype (1932), takes a different approach in that the serifs are more thickened terminals than separate strokes, tending towards the look of a humanist lineale, but the effect is still to suggest the stone-carved inscription rather than writing. Curiously, Albertus has found favour from time to time as a face for food packaging (for example, Cadbury's chocolate in the 1930s), the very opposite of the timelessness of its design root. Friz Quadrata, by Ernst Friz for ITC and released in 1978, is typically ITC – a very high x-height gives a curious distortion of the glyphic form; in the lower case the flaring stroke on bowls and on the spine of the "s" catches the eye and may impede readability. Gerard Unger's Amerigo of 1987, for Bitstream, is something of a hybrid, with similar tendencies towards high x-height as Quadrata, but slightly condensed. The more authentic glyphic is Trajan, 1989, by Carol Twombly, which takes the lettering of Trajan's column in Rome – a set of capitals that has been literally a touchstone for many type designers over the years – and produces a highly refined cut.

# Script

*Abefgør*

Snell Roundhand

## Snell Roundhand

*abcdefghijklmnopqrstuvwxyz*
*ABCDEFGHIJKLMNOPQRSTUVWXYZ*
*1234567890*

## Shelley Andante

*abcdefghijklmnopqrstuvwxyz*
*ABCDEFGHIJKLMNOPQRSTUVWXYZ*
*1234567890*

## Coronet

*abcdefghijklmnopqrstuvwxyz*
*ABCDEFGHIJKLMNOPQRSTUVWXYZ*
*1234567890*

## Mistral

*abcdefghijklmnopqrstuvwxyz*
*ABCDEFGHIJKLMNOPQRSTUVWXYZ*
*1234567890*

A wide-ranging group that is drawn together around the idea that the typeface is an imitation of handwriting. The florid twirls of Robert Hunter Middleton's Coronet (1937) can be seen to ape a fine hand, but Roger Excoffon's Choc (1955) and Mistral (1953) are more painterly, Mistral being remarkable for the manner in which the lower-case joins up. Excoffon's brush-technique arguably moves the fonts right out of script and into the broad stylized area that so many contemporary faces fall into. Matthew Carter's Snell Roundhand (1965) also manages some effective junctions and takes as its basis the work of the seventeenth-century writing master Charles Snell (his rules for consistency in writing help the product to be imitated in type). Carter's 1972 Shelley Script, also for Linotype, came in three exotically named variations – Allegro, Andante and Volante – which referred to the degree of calligraphic flourish involved. Hermann Zapf's Chancery for ITC (1979) was an altogether more restrained and readable face that has proven popular, while still displaying pen-drawn inflections.

# Black-letter

## Abefgor

Fette Fraktur

---

### Fette Fraktur

abcdefghijklmnopqrstuvwxyz
ABCDEFGHIJKLMNOPQRSTUVWXYZ
1234567890

---

### Goudy Text

abcdefghijklmnopqrstuvwxyz
ABCDEFGHIJKLMNOPQRSTUVWXYZ
1234567890

---

### Wittenburger Fraktur

abcdefghijklmnopqrstuvwxyz
ABCDEFGHIJKLMNOPQRSTUVWXYZ
1234567890

---

### Wilhelm Klingspor

abcdefghijklmnopqrstuvwxyz
ABCDEFGHIJKLMNOPQRSTUVWXYZ
1234567890

The original of movable type forms – the type style Gutenberg derived from the manuscript tradition – black-letter would seem an impossible distance from ever reclaiming in display or text the dominant position that it once held across Europe and retained in Germany until between the wars. Now it tends to be used only as a stylized and near unreadable flourish, giving a nod to tradition for a newspaper masthead. What better proof could there be of the 1990s maxim "we read best what we read most"? There are four principle groupings of black-letter – fraktur, textura, bastarda (Schwabacher) and rotunda. Fette Fraktur is from 1867–72, Offenbach, designer unknown. Heavy and yet with a romantic flourish, it suggests a freely drawn pen stroke. Wittenburger Fraktur is a variation on the angular but flowing form of fraktur. In contrast, Goudy Text is a textura, displaying more fixed angles but still taken as if from the movement of the pen, although Frederic Goudy's 1928 design for Monotype is inspired by the 42-line bible of Gutenberg. Wilhelm Klingspor is a highly ornamental textura by Rudolf Koch, for the Klingspor foundry in Offenbach, 1920–26. It features exaggerated terminal flourishes, and in the hairy effect this gives the final type, one can see a source for such a modern experimental face as Jesus Loves You (see page 160).

## Decorative

# Aefgor

Cooper Black

### Broadway

abcdefghijklmnopqrstuvwxyz
ABCDEFGHIJKLMNOPQRSTUVWXYZ
1234567890

### Arnold Böcklin

abcdefghijklmnopqrstuvwxyz
ABCDEFGHIJKLMNOPQRSTUVWXYZ
1234567890

### Cooper Black

abcdefghijklmnopqrstuvwxyz
ABCDEFGHIJKLMNOPQRSTUVWXYZ
1234567890

### Copperplate Gothic

ABCDEFGHIJKLMNOPQRSTUVWXYZ
ABCDEFGHIJKLMNOPQRSTUVWXYZ
1234567890

It sounds like a loose term, and it is – but how do we describe the rapidly increasing number of fonts that do not draw on one particular historical tradition or form of production, but are distinguished by being sports that draw on the varied visual culture of their time? The flagrant borrowings of visual form from aesthetic tendency can explain such fonts as Arnold Böcklin, which is emblematic of Art Nouveau (but this font also draws on black-letter). Frederic Goudy's Copperplate Gothic of 1902 is actually a highly functional design (holding up as a crisp form in small sizes on titling cards and the like). Its purpose, though, would seem to be decorative, if not its construction. Cooper Black is a loud character of a display type, designed 1921–5 by Oswald B. Cooper, sometimes very in but often out of fashion ever since. Like Morris Fuller Benton's Broadway of 1929, a dramatically contrasting quasi-geometric design that comes from but also helps define the American Art Deco aesthetic, Cooper Black has intimations of calligraphic origins but is clearly drawn. And perhaps it is this factor – the notion of letters being carefully assembled to wear a particular look or idiosyncrasy – that marks a group here, albeit these faces could also be put into other groups relating to the presence of serifs, or the intimation of cut letters with Copperplate Gothic.

# Abefgor

Blur

abcdefghijklmnopqrstuvwxyz
ABCDEFGHIJKLMNOPQRSTUVWXYZ
1234567890

Beowolf

abcdefghijklmnopqrstuvwxyz
ABCDEFGHIJKLMNOPQRSTUVWXYZ
1234567890

Trixie

abcdefghijklmnopqrstuvwxyz
ABCDEFGHIJKLMNOPQRSTUVWXYZ
1234567890

Exocet

ABCDEFGHIJKLMNOPQRSTUVWXYZ
1234567890

Note that terrible label on this classification: contemporary... what overblown rock music became called in the 1970s shortly before punk tried to flush it away. However, 1990s fonts have become increasingly hard to classify and show up the inadequacies of classification systems. The analysis largely followed over the previous pages was generally accepted until the 1980s. It mixes historical, formalist and even intentionalist readings of type (who says a type is supposed to be script?). These help us understand some connections, but they miss and even obscures other links. Can the thousands of new digital fonts find their place within the existing analysis? It has become impossible to do this, but just what will replace the old structure is uncertain. Type companies have failed to produce credible groupings in their catalogues. For example, is Blur, 1992, by Neville Brody a geometric sans serif, albeit a bit fuzzy? Fontshop International call it "amorphous", but it has links with Trixie, also 1991 by Erik van Blokland, in the same group, which gets dubbed an "ironic". And both link with Beowolf, by Blokland and Just van Rossum, 1990, which with its random changes is dubbed an "intelligents" font. Jonathan Barnbrook's Exocet from Emigre Fonts, 1994, has black irony in its name, but draws inspiration from Greek stone carving. Ironic glyphic, then? The serifs and hard geometry (note the U or Y) would tax a stone cutter, lacking some kind of refined power tool. In the opposite column, we come to a provocative conclusion.

# Abefgor

Template Gothic

---

## Template Gothic

abcdefghijklmnopqrstuvwxyz
ABCDEFGHIJKLMNOPQRSTUVWXYZ
1234567890

---

## Emigre Ten

abcdefghijklmnopqrstuvwxyz

ABCDEFGHIJKLMNOPQRSTUVWXYZ

1234567890

---

## OCR-A

abcdefghijklmnopqrstuvwxyz
ABCDEFGHIJKLMNOPQRSTUVWXYZ
1234567890

---

## New Alphabet

The faces on this page have forms heavily influenced by technologies. Barry Deck's Template Gothic, 1990, is from laundromat sign lettering; Emigre Ten is one of Zuzana Licko's early Emigre fonts that explored the bitmap; OCR-A is a design driven by engineers looking for computer-readable type; Wim Crouwel's New Alphabet of 1967 reduced letterforms to minimal structures suitable for an early computerised photocomposition system. But as New Alphabet has been digitised, made into a useable face for the 1990s by The Foundry, and as OCR-A has become a fashion item, and as Template Gothic and Emigre Ten are filed for a late 1980s/early 1990s revival due along soon, so we have to reconsider the terms of description – the faces clearly draw on technological contexts, and are in histories. But it is apparent that to map the location of a typeface, to pin it down in history and in formal properties, requires a system of multiple criteria, plotting the nature of a design on more than one axis. It is no longer credible to propose a closed system of classification, because we can now see that the creative nature of the subject determines that new forms will seek to step outside existing structures. There is no rule book, only a series of possible readings to be made of each new font and from which its coordinates may be plotted. But these are never fixed. There was once one 42-line printed bible, but there is no longer a bible for classification, if there ever was. And should we miss it? We can just remember what we like... and then ask why.

## Glossary

Note: some terms relating to characters and type groups are explained on preceding pages.

**Baseline**
The line (not printed) on which letters tend to sit and align. Descenders fall below this line.

**Bezier curves**
Curves created by drawing lines in relation to a series of coordinates. At the heart of the *PostScript* page description language.

**Bitmap**
The dots that make up a *digital* image. Digital typefaces have a bitmap image for screen display, each size having a separate cluster of bitmap information. This screen bitmap is low-resolution, and an accompanying printer font in high-resolution information, encoded in a form such as *PostScript*, enables the generation of a high-quality output.

**Black-letter**
Typefaces that are based on the gothic, medieval script. Textura, Fraktura, Old English, Rotunda and Bastarda (or Schwabacher) are groups of black-letter faces.

**Body type**
The type used for a main text, as opposed to headline or display usage; also known as text type. It is most often seen in sizes between 6 and 14 point.

**CD-Rom**
Compact disc, read-only memory. In the 1990s, type libraries have been transferred complete on to CDs capable of being read by computers with CD drives. Several thousand faces may be in a library and accessible to view, but users only have to buy faces as and when they need them; this is possible through the use of codes that unlock just those faces on the disc that a user wants to pay for. Online search engines on the internet with payment systems seem likely increasingly to replace CD-Rom technology as a way of promoting and distributing fonts.

**Chase**
The metal frame in which the *galleys* of metal type were locked as pages ready for printing or for a *stereotype* plate to be taken.

**Cold type**
Printing which is not produced by the *hot-metal* process, but involves the use of *founders' type, photosetting* or electronic processes.

**Colour**
In typography this can apply to purely monochrome pages, as it refers to the density of black/grey/white generated by the mass of type on the page. Choice of type, line length, leading, tracking – all these factors and others can affect the colour of the type.

**Composition**
The process of assembling individual characters of type into set matter of words, sentences and pages. This can be done by hand, *hot-metal* machine, *photosetting* or electronically through *digital* information.

**Condensed**
A typeface is condensed when the character form is compressed to a narrower width than is normal; the opposite is extended (or expanded). New technology of the *photosetting* and computer era enables characters to be condensed or extended by machine rather than specially *cut* as was required with metal setting.

**CRT**
Cathode ray tube, the technology central to television projection which also has an important part in the development of image-setting systems for type. Initial digital typesetting systems used a CRT to generate the type image as a series of pixels (picture elements) that were exposed on to a light-sensitive film, as with *photosetting*. *Laser setting* has now superseded CRT as the prime technology behind typesetting/image-setting. CRTs have been central to the display (and hence evolution) of screen type in the age of television and the personal computer. LCD (liquid crystal display) and other screen technologies are starting to replace the CRT, but the move to a radically higher resolution screen is still awaited.

**Cut**
Often used to define a particular font; a term dating from the days when a design was cut into a punch that was then used to form the matrices from which individual pieces of type were struck.

**Digital**
The term for the electronic technology that has taken over print and image manipulation systems since the 1980s. At the root of all the computer systems is the notion of sorting information digitally, as a mass of binary data.

**DPI**
Dots per inch, usually applied to output devices, such as printers and image-setters, to define the resolution of the image that is available. Dot matrix printers have a low dpi, hence the visibility of the dots and the crudeness of the resulting characters and graphics. Inkjet delivers higher resolution, and laser higher still. Rapid developments in printer technology mean that even a cheap personal computer printer offers 300 dpi or greater. High-end systems for quality reproduction, as in book printing, are in excess of 2000 dpi. The resolution seen on a personal computer screen, however, is equivalent to 72dpi.

**Dry transfer**
Process behind the development of companies in the 1960s such as Letraset and Mecanorma, where sheets of lettering were sold as transfers to be rubbed down and transferred as ready-made artwork, replacing the need for some setting. Originally the system was wet transfer, a messier and more awkward process.

**DTP**
Desktop publishing, the computerized design and production of print that was made possible by the introduction of small, low-cost computer systems offering a *wysiwyg* screen image that enabled designers to work on screen effectively. It has been available from the early 1980s.

**Electrotype**
A printing plate formed by the electrolytic deposition of copper on a wax mould of the original printing plate. See also *stereotype*.

**Em**
A unit of measurement that is normally the square of a given point size of type. It is based on the letter "m", which tends to form a square piece of type, its width the same as the height of the face.

**En**
A unit of measurement half the width of an *em*.

**Extended/expanded**
Terms to describe the stretching of a typeface to a larger width than the normal dimensions of characters; the opposite is *condensed*.

**Family**
In type, a term given to a range of typeface designs that are all variations on one central design. Principal variations are roman, italic, bold, light, condensed and extended/expanded.

**Font/Fount**
The meaning has changed over time; the current usage defines the complete character set of a particular typeface in a particular size and style.

**Founders'/foundry type**
Setting based on the use of precast metal characters of type composed by hand from a tray of type.

**Foundry**
The place of manufacture for type, dating from the days when a type foundry was a place for serious metalwork. Now sometimes used to describe the small digital type studio/distributor.

**Furniture**
As in "page furniture", those regular elements of a layout that are not type, but are part of the typographic arrangement, such as rules and bars, fleurons and the like.

**Galley**
Strip of set type, either in hot metal when arranged on the *stone* or as a bromide strip output from *photosetting* or image-setting.

**Half-tone**
Blocks or pieces of film converted from images into a form ready for printing. They consist of a greater or lesser number of dots that depict light and dark areas.

**Hardware**
The physical machinery in computer systems, as opposed to the *software*, which is the particular operating system and the other *programs* carried on the equipment. The CPU (central processing unit) is at the heart of any system, with the screen and printer being described as peripherals.

**Hinting**
A function within digital type, whereby a range of automatic adjustments are made to simplify and clarify characters when they are produced in very small sizes or on low-resolution output. These adjustments guide the output so that it retains key characteristics. Most, but not all, digital fonts were hinted, but the development of Adobe Type Manager software in part decreased the need for hinting.

**Hot metal**
Term for type and the printing process that involves casting type from hot metal in order to print.

**Inline/outline**
Characters are inlined when part of the character stroke is cut away to create a white area within the letter other than a bowl. They are outlined when a line is put on the outside edge to create an open aspect to the form. This is different from adding a shadow effect, although they may be combined.

**Justification**
The ranging of type on both left and right sides; see also *ranged left* and *ranged right*.

**Kerning**
The spacing of letters closer than is standard, usually in order to create the optical effect of consistency of space between characters by allowing part of one letter to "kern" into the white space of another; see also *tracking*.

**Laser setting**
Lasers fire flashes of light according to the information of the character outline (which could be *PostScript* encoded, or some other page description, or *bitmap*). This light either records an image on a light-sensitive surface (laser typesetters/image-setters), or generates an electrostatically charged image that is put directly on to paper (laser printers). The former have high resolution, the latter lower resolution.

**Leading**
The space between lines. Prior to photocomposition, this was created by physically inserting a strip of metal called a lead into the page make-up in order to give more white space between the lines of type.

**Legibility**
In typography, legibility and readability are two terms that have precise and separate meanings. Legibility is usually taken to mean the quality of distinction between characters – the clarity of the individual letters. Readability is the quality of reading provided by a piece of typography, in which kerning, leading and other factors will have a bearing on the function of the type.

**Letterspacing**
The insertion of greater than normal spacing between characters.

**Ligature**
The joining of two or more letters for optical purposes (as with æ, fl or fi), a feature common in metal setting but less so with *photosetting*, where the enlarged character set thus required is undesirable for the manufacturers. There are signs, however, that ligatures are returning with digital typography.

**Linotype**
Describes a company, machine, system and type library. Linotype was the original hot-metal system, launched in 1886, and involved the setting of a line of type in hot metal by an operator working a keyboard directly attached to the setting machine. In contrast, the *Monotype* machine set one character at a time.

**Lithography**
Printing process that works on the principle of having an image on metal (or, originally, stone), parts of which will take ink, and parts of which (those not intended to print) reject ink; the surface to be printed is placed against this lithographic image. Water can be used to create the process of the attraction and repelling of ink. Offset lithography is where the image is first offset on to another surface (the "blanket") and this then transfers on to the surface to be printed.

**Matrix**
In metal setting, the mould from which the type is cast; it carries an impression of the type character which has been struck from the *punch*; it is made from copper or brass. In *photosetting*, the term used for the grid of characters that often carries the character set of a face.

**Mechanical composition**
The process of selecting and arranging type by machine rather than by hand. Prior to the *Linotype* and *Monotype* machines at the end of the nineteenth century, there was no commercially viable method of mechanical setting that could select, cast and re-sort (or melt down) type.

**Monospace**
A term applied to those typefaces, such as typewriter faces, where each character is allotted the same space.

**Monotype**
A company, machine, system and type library developed in the 1890s shortly after the *Linotype*. It offered a system based on setting individual pieces of type in hot metal, following instructions punched into a spool of tape by a keyboard operator. Monotype has been associated with the development of a fine type library, along with later type and print technology.

**Multiple masters**
Technology developed by Adobe Systems that allows the generation of a wide variety of fonts from one typeface – condensed and extended, or light and bold, even serif to sans serif. The software takes up a comparatively small amount of computer memory, providing a sophisticated range of options on relatively small systems at much lower costs than buying all the fonts. The first faces, Myriad and Minion, were launched early in 1992.

**OCR**
Optical character recognition; OCR devices can scan, or read, type so that it can be processed by computer. From the late 1950s onwards the issue of machine-readable faces has been important; this led to specially designed faces, as well as being related to the development of scanning technology.

**Offset lithography**
See *lithography*.

**Outline**
See *inline/outline*.

**Pantograph**
An instrument capable of transferring a design by tracing the master drawing. Linn Boyd Benton's pantographic *punchcutter* made it easier to convert a design for type on to the *punch* and made possible the development of *mechanical composition*.

**Photosetting/phototypesetting**
The setting of type by exposing the image of a type character on to light-sensitive film, with the photosetter outputting a bromide that is then used for paste-up on a page. The resulting artwork, when proofed and combined with other graphics, goes through a further film process to generate plates for offset *lithography*.

**Pica**
Typographical measurement comprising 12 points and thus amounting to roughly $\frac{1}{6}$ of an inch; also formerly the term applied to 12 point type.

**Point**
Typographical measurement; in the US and UK it is 0.0138 of an inch or 0.351mm; in Continental Europe it is 0.346mm.

**PostScript**
The digital page description language developed by Adobe Systems and widely adopted as a standard for digital page software. It is device- and resolution-independent, requiring only a PostScript-compatible system, and is thus able to work on a wide range of equipment. Type is described in a series of mathematical formulae that generate *Bezier curves* which are then filled in with dots to the output-system resolution.

**Press**
The printing machine, so-called because it traditionally works by pressing a piece of paper against the surface carrying the image, whether a relief image of metal type or a rubber blanket carrying an offset lithographic image. For each colour a separate plate exists and a separate impression is made. A flatbed press carries the image on a flat surface at the base and moves the paper against it, while a rotary press wraps the image as a plate round a rotating drum under which is passed the surface to be printed.

**Program**
The computer software carrying the instructions and operating methods of a particular system. A typesetting program has to be loaded on the hardware – the computerized equipment – before it can work as a typesetter.

**Punch**
Metal bar containing the master design of a type character used for striking a *matrix* for casting the type for printing.

**Punchcutter**
The highly skilled craftsman who physically inscribed the design of a typeface on to the metal bars of the *punch*. Prior to the *pantograph* this was a job of such individual skill that the punchcutter was often the same as the type designer, or was regarded as contributing to the design.

**Ranged left**
Ranging of type at the left side, leaving the right side ragged; also called unjustified. See *justification*.

**Ranged right**
Ranging of type at the right side, leaving the left side ragged; such a setting is unjustified. See *justification*.

**Readability**
See *legibility*.

**Reversed out**
Type which is the unprinted area, standing out of black or a coloured background.

**RIP**
Raster image processor. Device for converting ("rastering") the information from, say, a *PostScript* encryption into a series of dots, produced to a density determined by the output device.

**Software**
Programs in computer systems carrying typefaces and other typographic information, as well as the programs within which type will be worked with (such as QuarkXPress or Fontographer) and the operating system of the computer itself. They work on the system hardware, such as the central processing unit and the printer.

**Stereotype**
A duplicate metal plate made from a relief printing plate by taking an impression in a soft material (such as papier-mâché plate) and then casting the duplicates from this mould. This was often the process for converting a page of set matter into a plate suitable for printing.

**Stone**
The flat surface on which metal type was imposed (laid out) before being tightened up in the *chase* ready for printing or plating.

**Stress**
The angle of thickening across a curved letter. For example, modern faces are distinguished by a pronounced vertical stress, whereas humanist faces have an inclined backward-sloping stress, imitative of a pen-drawn character.

**Swash**
The flourish that may extend a stroke or replace a serif on a letter; characters with fancy flourishes are known as swash letters.

**Tracking**
The spacing standard set between characters in a text. *Photosetting* and digital setting made it much easier to play with tracking, either "negative" tracking, where characters have closer *kerning*, or "positive" tracking, whereby a word, line or text is given *letterspacing*. Digital typography introduced even greater flexibility into the manipulation of character relationships.

**Wysiwyg**
What you see is what you get; computer systems that reproduce on screen a working simulation of the graphic information that could be output by the system.

**Notes**

Letters of Introduction

1 Jan Tschichold in *The New Typography*, 1928, translated from *Die Neue Typographie* by Ruari McLean, University of California Press, 1995.

2 El Lissitzky in *Unovis No. 1*, as translated by Patricia Railing in *More About 2 Squares*, Artists Bookworks, 1990.

3 Yve Alain-Bois, from *Formless*, Zone Books, 1997.

4 Neil Postman, from *Amusing Ourselves To Death*, Viking Penguin, 1985.


**1910**

1 Filippo Marinetti, translated in *Futurismo e Futurismi*, Bompiani, 1986.

2 Filippo Marinetti, translated in *Marinetti: Selected Writings*, edited by R.W. Flint, Secker & Warburg, 1972.


**1920**

1 László Moholy-Nagy, in *Staatliches Bauhaus, Weimar, 1919-23*, translated in *Bauhaus 1919–28*, catalogue edited by Herbert Bayer, Walter Gropius and Ise Gropius, The Museum Of Modern Art, 1938.

**1930**

1 The complete text of this speech from 18 April 1959 was reprinted in *Print* magazine, volume 18, number one, 1964; also in Ruari McLean, *Jan Tschichold: Typographer*, Lund Humphries, 1975.

**1940**

1 Jan Tschichold, "Glaube und Wirklichkeit", *Schweizer Graphische Mitteilungen*, June 1946, translated as "Belief and Reality" in Ruari McLean, *Jan Tschichold: Typographer*, Lund Humphries, 1975.


**1950**

1 Information from *Advertiser's Weekly*, quoted in Kenneth Day, *The Typography of Press Advertisement*, Ernest Benn, 1956.


**1970**

1 Adrian Frutiger, *Der Mensch und seine Zeichen*, Weiss Verlag, 1978, translated as *Signs and Symbols: their Design and Meaning*, Studio Editions, 1989.

2 Paula Scher, quoted in Hugh Aldersey-Williams, *New American Design*, Rizzoli.


**1980**

1 Matthew Carter, *PC Computing*, January 1989.

2 Grafix National Conference survey, reported in *U&lc*, summer 1991.

3 Matthew Carter, *Communication Arts*, January–February 1989.

## Bibliography

If you have read this far, you might want to head off for in-depth coverage of a particular movement, technology, individual or perhaps something altogether more lateral. An exhaustive list covering all the subjects and issues touched on in these pages would be... exhausting, for reader and writer alike. So here is a relatively brief, eclectic list. These recommendations are in part complementary, in part contradictory, and some are just personal favourites. They often contain extensive bibliographies.

### Books

*Printing Types*
D.B. Updike (second edition, Harvard University Press, Cambridge, Massachusetts, 1937, republished Dover Publications, 1980). A seminal earlier history.

*An Introduction to Bibliography*
Philip Gaskell (Oxford University Press, Oxford, 1972). Excellent on the history of letterpress printing and the making of books. Note appendix on Elizabethan handwriting which illustrates the evolution of letterform.

*The Elements of Typographic Style*
Robert Bringhurst (Hartley & Marks, Vancouver, 1992/1996). Immensely knowledgeable (written by a practising typographer and poet) and yet often infuriating in its presentation of "rules". Question it to death.

*Modern Typography*
Robin Kinross (Hyphen Press, London, 1992). An intelligent and opinionated essay on the nature of the "modern". Part of being modern is to eschew colour pictures and insist on the unending quest for rationalism. Stimulating.

*Anatomy of a Typeface*
Alexander Lawson (David R. Godine/Hamish Hamilton, Lincoln, Massachusetts/London, 1990). Avuncular trawl through the history of many classics.

*Letters of Credit:*
*A View of Type Design*
Walter Tracy
(Gordon Fraser, London, 1986). Another personal guide.

*Die Neue Typographie*
Jan Tschichold (Berlin, 1928; fac-simile reprint Brinkman & Bose, Berlin, 1987; English translation as *The New Typography*, translator Ruari McLean, University of California Press, 1995). An attempt to summarize the 1920s innovations in one small book... and a highly influential one.

*Type, Sign, Symbol*
Adrian Frutiger (ABC Verlag, Zurich, 1980). Type in its mark-making context from the creator of the Univers.

*An Essay on Typography*
Eric Gill (second edition, Dent, London, 1936). Characterful, quirky, brief.

*Dimensional Typography*
J. Abbott Miller (A Kiosk Report/Princeton Architectural Press, 1996). Intriguing proposals of three-dimensional forms from previously two-dimensional type.

*Stop Stealing Sheep & Find Out How Type Works*
Erik Spiekermann and E.M. Ginger (Adobe Press, 1993). Witty guide to recent practice.

*Typography*
*on the Personal Computer*
Sumner Stone (Lund Humphries, London, 1991). Interesting to read in the light of subsequent developments.

*The Monotype Recorder:*
*One Hundred Years of Type Making 1897–1997*
(Monotype Typography, 1997). Useful summary that gives another slant on the period and subject through the history of one key company.

*Pioneers of Modern Typography*
Herbert Spencer (second edition, Lund Humphries, London, 1982). A few key designers are elevated to heroic status.

*Frederic Goudy*
D.J.R. Bruckner (Harry N. Abrams, New York, 1990). Human interest through words.

*Alfabeta:*
*Lo Studio e Il Disegno del Carattere*
Aldo Novarese (Progresso Grafico, Turin, 1965/83). Human interest through drawings.

*Typography: a Manual of Design*
Emil Ruder (Arthur Niggli, Teufen AR, Switzerland, 1967). A Swiss style.

*About Alphabets*
Hermann Zapf (MIT Press, Cambridge, Massachusetts, 1970).

*The Graphic Designer and His Design Problems*
Josef Müller Brockmann (Arthur Niggli, Teufen AR, Switzerland, 1983). Perhaps the most revered of the Swiss style masters.

*Moholy-Nagy*
Krisztina Passuth (Thames & Hudson, London, 1985).

*Amusing Ourselves to Death:*
*Public Discourse in the Age of Show Business*
Neil Postman (Viking Penguin, New York, 1985). A sobering analysis that suggests our literacy has moved beyond (or backwards) from joined-up sentences.

*The Gutenberg Galaxy:*
*Making of Typographic Man*
Marshall McLuhan (Toronto University Press, Toronto, 1962). It didn't make much sense... and then it did.

*Being Digital*
Nicholas Negroponte (Basic Books, New York, 1995).

### Annuals

The Type Directors Club in New York and the Tokyo Typodirectors Club both have well-produced and usually stimulating annuals. Also dig out old Penrose Annuals, a faithful record of printing industry innova-tion for over 80 years from 1895.

### Magazines

*Emigre*, 4475 D Street, Sacramento, CA 95819, USA. <www.emigre.com>. Essential if sometimes painful reading for the contemporary typographer.

*Fuse*, Unit 2, Whitehorse Yard, 78 Liverpool Road, London, N1 0QD, England. Consistently innovative in its themed packs of new fonts, posters and a booklet. Distributed by Fontshop International worldwide and FontWorks in England. Or <http://www.research.co.uk/fuse/fuse-home.html>

*Creative Review*, 50 Poland Street, London, W1V 4AX, England. More typographic context than kerning tips... but the magazine and CD-Rom are your platform as well as information source. Note my personal bias here.

*U&lc*, 228 East 45th Street, New York, NY 10017, USA. The ITC/Letraset promo magazine is also widely read, diverse in subject matter and design.

*Idea*, Seibundo-Shinkosha, 1-13-7 Yayoicho, Nakanoku, Tokyo 164, Japan. What's hot in the West from a sharp Japanese viewpoint.

*Seybold*. The Seybold series of reports and conferences provide an expert running commentary on the development of digital publishing. <seyboldreport.com>

*Octavo* 1986–1992. Produced by the design group 8vo and now ended. Just eight issues (the last one a CD-Rom), so very much a collector's item. Read them as a manifesto for respecting the modern.

### Type manufacturers and software companies

Catalogues, CD-Roms and online information are the primary way of finding out the choice in type today – information that is usually free. Online catalogues for browsing and downloading fonts are increasingly prevalent, with search engines that advance – or at least provide alter-natives – to conventional systems of tracking down a typeface.

Monotype Typography, Salfords, Redhill, Surrey RH1 5JP, England.

Emigre, Inc. As for the magazine above.

FontShop International, Bergmannstrasse 102, D-10961 Berlin, Germany. <www.fontfont.de>

Adobe Systems, Inc., 1585 Charleston Road, PO Box 7900, Mountain View, CA 94039-7900, USA. <www.adobe.com/prodin-dex/webtype/>

Microsoft. Contact through <www.asia.microsoft.com/open-type/>. Given the company's power, Microsoft's typography group could become the most influential (but not necessarily the best) typographers in the world. Check out what they might be thinking here.

Apple Computer. <www.apple.com>. This large web-site has a useful search engine up front which will give you thousands of matches for terms like "typogra-phy" or "TrueType". Be specific.

The Foundry, Studio 12, 10–11 Archer Street, London, W1V 7HG, England. Producers of the Architype series of fonts, digital re-creations of "classic" avant garde typefaces.

### Futures

The consortium running the World Wide Web. Links here to important papers, develop-ments about the basic history, structure and technology of the web, including information on hypertext and Ted Nelson.

### And for more

Try keying "typography" into a search engine on the internet. On 3/2/98 the Hotbot search engine presented 45,999 matches. There will most probably be many more by now. Refine search terms and you might find something useful.

Published 1998 by Gingko Press Inc.
5768 Paradise Drive, Suite J
Corte Madera, CA 94925, USA
email: gingko@linex.com

Gingko Press Verlag GmbH
Hamburger Strasse 180
22083 Hamburg, Germany
email: gingkopress@t-online.de

Published by arrangement with Laurence King Publishing

This book was produced by Calmann & King Ltd, London

ISBN 3-927258-89-X

Designed by Angus Hyland assisted by Simon Piehl

Printed in Singapore

**Lewis Blackwell** wrote this book. He also wrote *The End of Print* (about the work of David Carson) and its sequel *2ndsight*. With Neville Brody he produced *G1*. He was last seen working with Scott and Laurie Makela on a new survey of graphic design, *Whereishere*, for which he was reading up on the history and theory of pornography and world religions, among other things. He is the editor and publisher of *Creative Review*, the leading magazine (and CD-Rom) on the communication arts. His daughter is called Caledonia, modified Scottish.

**Angus Hyland** designed this book and many other things. Since April 1998 he has been a partner at Pentagram, London. Hyland designed the 1950s divider with Simon Piehl.

**Irma Boom**, who created the 1920s divider, works mainly on books. She goes beyond the conventions of design, being involved at the concept stage, and also in research, authorship and editing. Between 1991 and 1996 she designed and co-edited a 2,136-page book weighing 3.5 kilograms on the 100th anniversary of a major company. She has had her own studio in Amsterdam, lectures widely, and is a visiting professor at Yale University.

**Cyan** is a Berlin-based group of designers, founded in 1992 by Daniela Haufe, Sophie Alex and Detlef Fiedler. They work chiefly for cultural and governmental institutions and are united in a respect and reference for the twentieth-century avant garde. They aim to "maintain the idea of reading as an occupation directed at the gaining of experience" and believe "reading needs engagement and awareness" which leads them to oppose "fast-food communication". The 1940s divider is their work.

**Naomi Enami** lives and works in Tokyo. He has created images on computer since the late 1980s (the divider he was asked to produce). Prior to this he was a magazine art director on leading magazines including *Elle* and *Marie Claire* in Japan. He works with his design company Digitalogue.

**Vince Frost** runs his own studio, Frost Design, in London and Tokyo. He has won many awards internationally, particularly for art direction on *Big* magazine and *The Independent* magazine. Recent clients include the Royal Mail, Sony and Magnum. "I have a strong interest in wood and metal type, anything dusty and dirty. I prefer to use three-dimensional type rather than electronic. So when I have a new job I visualize piles of trays of forgotten type. It's much more of a physical process." As things were in 1900, for which he designed the divider. In 1998 he was the launch art director for Japanese *Vogue*.

**Graphic Thought Facility** are Paul Neale and Andrew Stevens. Graduates of the Royal College of Art, they formed GTF in 1990 and are based in London. Their (joint) top five typefaces of all time are currently: 1, the Sony logotype; 2, Schriebmaschinenshrift; 3, Bunny Ears; 4, Girl; 5, Souvenir Monospace. They art directed the 1970s remix, with design and craft by Lizzie Finn, a freelance graphic designer.

**Fernando Gutierrez** is a founder of the Barcelona studio Grafica. He once designed an issue of *Colors* magazine with 359 pictures but only 442 words. He gave no words for this, but did create the 1910 divider.

**Chip Kidd's** book jacket designs for Alfred A. Knopf have featured in numerous magazines and won many awards. Descriptions include "Monstrously ugly" (John Updike), "Apparently obvious" (William Boyd) and "Faithful flat-earth rendering" (Don DeLillo). Kidd has also written widely about graphic design and popular culture and is the author of his own book, *Batman Collected* (Titan, 1996) in which he attempts to rid himself of his inner demons. To no avail – he is the co-author and designer of *Batman Animated* (HarperCollins, 1998). Batman was created in the 1930s – for which Kidd did the divider here.

**M+M** are Michael Amzalag and Mathias Augustyniak who have worked together in Paris since 1991 across many different kinds of media – books, fashion catalogues, stickers, art catalogues, towels, posters, record covers, advertising, magazines, postcards. "We spend our time trying to contaminate the world with our ideas. We do recommend to all readers to use Barthes/Simpson typeface (designed in 1994 by M+M and based on standardized McDonald french fries) to write their thoughts." M+M's contamination of this book is with the 1960s divider.

**Dirk van Dooren and Karl Hyde**, who created our 1990s divider, are two members of the London-based tomato collective of artists, whose output covers design, film, music and other media. Hyde is also a member of the music group Underworld.

**Acknowledgements:** many thanks to many people, including all the people mentioned in *20th Century Type*, plus Linda Jorgensen at Monotype Typography, David Quay and Freda Sack at The Foundry, FontShop International, Fontshop UK, Stuart Jensen of Fontworks UK, Neville Brody, David Carson, and especially the long-suffering editor of this book, Jo Lightfoot at Calmann & King.